GOLDEN OAK FURNITURE

Velma Susanne Warren

Revised price guide

Schiffer Publishing Ltd

W9-BNU-981

4880 Lower Valley Rd. Atglen, PA 19310 USA

Preface

Golden oak furniture has enjoyed an intense revival during recent years. Considerable quantities of the once-discarded "used furniture" has been retrieved and restored to again serve the needs and beautify the homes of modern American families. The golden oak adds its "glow," warming its surroundings as we approach the dawn of the 21st century.

In most cases, these oak treasures will remain with their new-found families to be passed along to future generations. The grown children of many parent collectors "put their names in" for the furnishings of Mom and Dad's home, which now has the status of heirloom. Oak furniture is respected, loved, admired, and avidly sought. Some serious collectors seem to have an insatiable appetite for the next glorious oak piece which possesses that "golden glow." To find a match is absolutely thrilling! The variety is endless, the pursuit invigorating! The warm, friendly, and glorious oak lives on....

The keyhole-shaped beveled mirror rests in a harp above the small, slightly swelled chest on shaped legs. $900

Introduction

Originally, photographs of the collection were used to help enthusiasts become aware of the variety of styles available in American turn-of-the-twentieth-century, oak furniture.

The photographs provided a means to visualize a particular "feeling" they sought as they developed their room settings. Whether a simple country decor or an elaborate one, plain or carved oak furniture could provide the desired atmosphere and sophisticated mood.

Many rooms and entire homes were furnished. The photographs, then cataloged by the customer's name, were used for reference in coordinating on-going additions to their collections. Design details of former purchases were compared with items currently available to provide complimentary suggestions. Knowing the taste of the collector and his future needs made it possible to provide furniture to help create their "oak dream rooms."

This piano stool is distinctive with its large rope-twisted center column, spindles, and legs which rest on glass ball and talon clawfeet. $400

The Age of Golden Oak

"Good OAK FURNITURE is more nearly 'boy-proof' than any other equally fine cabinet-wood."

Its elegance, dignity and artistic adaptability—are backed by its sturdy resistance to dents and scratches. (Really an important point.)

"There is no finer heirloom than good OAK furniture." There is no more *safe* and *enduring* investment—none better worth *insisting* upon.

AMERICAN OAK MFRS. ASSN., answers all letters. Address 1416, 14 Main St., Memphis, Tenn.

Initially manufactured in the 1860s, American oak furniture ascended to first place in popularity through the 1870s. Walnut furniture had previously reigned, but by the 1880s it was overcut and replaced by oak for furniture manufacturing.

The cultural needs of 19th century America spawned the oak furniture industry. Oak became the furniture manufacturer's dream. Huge virgin oak forests of the South and Midwest produced millions of board feet of lumber each year. Oak could be kiln dried and ready for use within weeks. Furniture factories sprung up wherever there was a stream or river to provide power.

Elaborate improvements had evolved in woodworking machinery during the 1870s and 1880s. Some of the machines displayed an almost human intelligence, turning out wood that would do credit to the hands of a skilled artist. Two marvelous machines to develop were the Goehring machine which enabled the working of geometric figures on wood, and a wood engraving machine which was patented to reproduce the human face or form, animals, and landscapes. Anything that could be drawn with a pencil could be produced on the surface of the wood. Furniture manufacturers invented machines capable of turning massive table legs, carving ornate scrollwork, cutting raised panels, pressing designs into chair backs, slicing thin veneers and turning

quantities of identical spindles simultaneously. The tough quality of the oak lumber allowed the wood to take the most intricate designs power machinery could impose upon it.

Another marvelous machine of the 1880s was the Knapp dovetailer. Available from the early 1870s, this scallop-and-dowel form of drawer joinery was used widely during the last two decades of the 19th century. The machine, made by the Knapp Dovetailing Machine Company of North Hampton, Massachusetts, won medals and awards at major exhibitions after 1873. Its improvements after 1881 made it possible for one operator to turn out two hundred drawers per day and elicited glowing testimonials from the furniture manufacturers.

The workers, however, had a much more restrained enthusiasm. They reasoned that new machinery endangered their jobs. A worker in Wisconsin earned an annual wage of $400 in 1889. A chair factory worker realized $100 less.

Strikes were threatened, as in Grand Rapids in 1884 when Berkey & Gay reduced the wages of employees who earned over $1.25 per day. But the strikes rarely materialized. One in four of the city's cabinetmakers was without work at the time and employment at any wage apparently seemed to be better than none.

During the 1880s, the principal centers for furniture manufacture were Chicago, specializing in parlor furniture; Cincinnati, specializing in dining and chamber (bedroom) pieces; and Grand Rapids specialized in **quality.** Other centers included Louisville, Kentucky; Indianapolis and Evansville, Indiana; Milwaukee and Sheboygan, Wisconsin; Rockford, Illinois and Jamestown, New York. It wasn't until 1888 that furniture production began in High Point, North Carolina.

By the end of the 1880s, the furniture industry had recovered from its earlier slump. Business boomed! Cincinnati was planning a major exhibition, the first of its kind in the United States, to show off the products of the city's 150 factories and 5000 furniture workers. In Rockford, a Manufacturers Palace was slated to open in 1891. Grand Rapids plants were operating at full capacity 12 to 13 hours per day to complete orders for the most lucrative season in furniture history.

Throughout the 1880s, new furniture lines were brought out every six months, sometimes with subtle changes in decoration. The chief incentive in design change was novelty or besting the competition. The selection waned in the 1890s when most manufacturers re-tooled only once a year.

When all the woodcarving was done by hand, only the wealthy could indulge in the extravagance of furniture so ornamented. But in this age of the machine, the furniture makers were able to supply their customers with the most elegant designs at a cost formerly charged for plain work. Distinctive, attractive, mass-produced, durable furniture resulted. So began the era of Golden Oak which reached its height in the 1890s and remaining through the early 1900s. It is now revived nearly a century later.

The oval mirror, suspended in a shaped S-scrolled harp hangs over the softly curved, 32" wide top of this vanity. It has original varnish, and is unrestored. The single drawer with oak button knobs rests above a curved apron and slightly tapered front legs. $950

The carved frame of this set of six dining chairs enhances the rose motif of its upholstery. Padded armrests add comfort to the two armchairs. The turned, tapered and twisted front legs rest upon castors to allow easy moving. $3,500

Entrance Hall

HALL SEATS

Beautifully designed, the "Snow White" oval, beveled mirror of this all seat is surrounded by shaped framing and elaborate, applied scroll carvings. $3,500

A long, shaped, beveled mirror with curved lines and applied scroll carvings decorate solid, quarter-sawn hall seat. A "slipper-box" is provided beneath the lift seat between the curved arms. $1,800

Deeply cut, scrolled carvings on an elliptical frame decorate this outstanding hall seat with beveled mirror (of selected, solid, quarter-sawn oak). Scrolls outline and decorate the back panel and a full-width lift seat rests between shaped arms and the feet. $2,600

The cut-out back panel of this hall seat and oval mirror are enhanced by the carved crest. Graceful arms and feet continue the flowing lines. $1,800

Elaborate carvings embellish the framing of this solid, quartered oak hall seat with bold style. $2,800

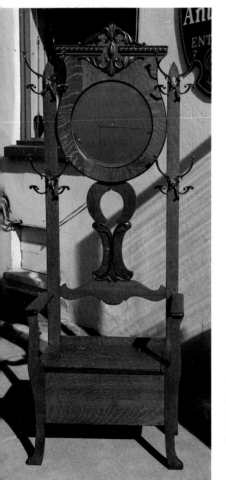

Slim in style, this hall seat resembles a keyhole. The small, round mirror hangs between double hat hooks. An umbrella stand is attached to the side. $950

This solid, quarter-sawn hall seat has an oval, beveled mirror set into recessed designs of the framing. The rounded top and carved, claw feet add elegance to the otherwise undecorated design. $1,600

The round, beveled mirror with carved crest rests on a cut-out back panel between two straight supporting posts on this hall seat. Simple in design, yet it possesses a strong character. $1,400

The oval, framed, beveled mirror hangs over the shaped back of this hall seat with a simple, but attractive, design. $1,600

A shaped and beveled mirror on this hall seat is enhanced by a curving frame and carved crest. The pierced back has an interesting center design. $2,000

Scrolled carvings accentuate the shaped, beveled mirror of this double hall seat. They swirl at the seven-feet-high crest, encircle the fancy hat hooks and decorate the back. The arms join the back to the lift seat with additional scrolls accenting the face of the "Boot box." (42" wide), $2,400

BENCHES

Benches of this style were used in libraries and other public buildings. The twenty curved slats and contoured seat are comfortable. Single post back legs bend to the floor. $800

This 40"-wide, solid quarter-sawn oak bench is petite. Its flowing lines and heart-shaped, cut-out back accented with applied scroll carvings. 35" tall and 14" deep, the seat displays its grain as it rests between two shapely end panels forming the feet and supporting the arms. $900

Twenty-three, slightly curved slats are enclosed between the rails of this four-foot bench. Solidly constructed, it rests square on the floor. $900

Triple panels add interest to the back of this 46" hall bench. Below its curved crest, solid, quartered oak side panels slope from the back to shape the arms with carved decoration on each end. The deep base panel enclose a storage area under a hinged seat. $1,000

Solid, quartered oak panels are particularly attractive in this hall bench. The lines are basically straight with a small carved medallion at center back. Small rolls decorate the arms and back. The base panel curves below the hinged seat where it meets the end panels. $1,000

Applied scroll carvings accent the back and face of this hall bench. Shaped arm posts and curved legs frame a storage area under the seat. This bench was found with a matching mirror (not shown). $1,500 set.

This solid, quartered oak, single-seat, hall bench, is petite. The rounded back and shaped side panels meet the hinged seat to create a storage space. $850

Solid quartered oak swirls around the deeply carved masque in the back of this single bench seat. $1,250

HAT RACKS-HALL TREES

Ball and tapered turnings decorate the column and legs of this hat rack. $450

A tall, turned column supports cast iron hooks and rests on widely spread, hoof feet. $425

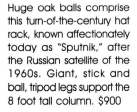

This Mission style hat rack incorporates an umbrella stand with a drip pan in the base. $400

Huge oak balls comprise this turn-of-the-century hat rack, known affectionately today as "Sputnik," after the Russian satellite of the 1960s. Giant, stick and ball, tripod legs support the 8 foot tall column. $900

Fancy brass hooks pivot at the top of the ring-turned column which is supported by legs with cloven feet. $450

MISCELLANEOUS

Taxidermy mountings of hunting trophies were popularly mounted on oak plaques. This eight-point buck is displayed on a most attractively carved and decorated wall board. Collection of Robert Stull. $400

The opened lid of this portable "potty" reveals an oak cover for the porcelain container. A small drawer is on the left. $300

This type of easel, with spindle-turned decoration, stood in a parlor to display a prized, family portrait. $175

Incised carvings surround the center, concave, translucent glass insert painted in oils. Unsigned by the artist. $750

The original tapestry and wood finish remain on this fireplace screen. $200

Scrolled feet and a quartered oak frame with beaded lower edge enhance tufted velour upholstery on this parlor couch, or "fainting sofa" as they are sometimes called. $1,500

Turned spindles encircle a brass drip pan on this umbrella stand with bentwood rings to support the umbrellas. $850

CLOCKS

A pendulum wall clock in an octagonal case is marked by the maker "Seth Thomas" on its white face. $500

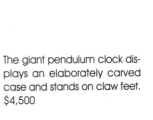

The giant pendulum clock displays an elaborately carved case and stands on claw feet. $4,500

This pendulum wall clock, marked "Regulator A" on the pendulum door, is housed in a decorated case. $800

Kitchen shelf clock with it's decorated pressed case and beaded trim houses what once was a "white faced" pendulum clock. The brass pendulum is at rest behind the decorated glass door. $250

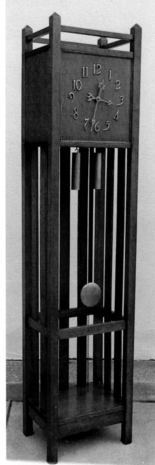

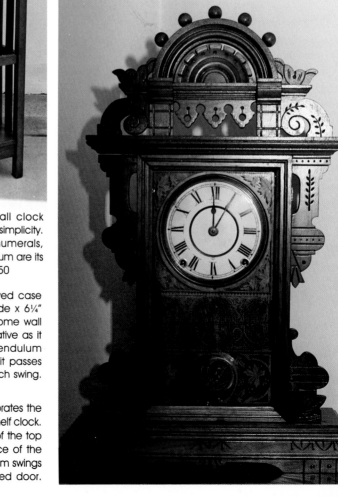

The Mission-style hall clock stands 78" tall in its simplicity. The brass hands, numerals, weights, and pendulum are its only decoration. $750

The elaborately carved case (45" high x 15½" wide x 6¼" deep) of this handsome wall clock is most decorative as it keeps time. The pendulum swings into view as it passes the peephole on each swing. $800

Incised carving decorates the case of this kitchen shelf clock. The domed design of the top crowns the white face of the clock as the pendulum swings behind the decorated door. $650

ROCKING CHAIRS

This rocker, though modestly decorated, offers a wide, deep form-fitting seat and high, curved back for comfort. Rockers of this style are constructed of multi-ply quarter-sawn oak veneer, selected for its highly figured grain. These rockers have come through the years exceptionally well if not subjected to dampness which would cause the plys to separate. $450

Beautifully detailed saddle seat rocker. The intricately pressed headpiece is supported by seven long, tapered spindles and turned backposts set into the seat. $475

Simply decorated rocker has incised carving to trim the finger-grip. Ten tapered spindles join the wide lower rail. Broad bent arms are most comfortable supported by four turned spindles and armpost. $550

Outstanding triple-pressed rocker with broad, intricately decorated headpiece. Nine twisted spindles join the shaped middle rail, accentuated by a shapely lower decorated rail below. The sideposts are elaborately turned, shaped, and fluted. The bent arms are supported by spiral spindles and large turned armposts. $900

Detail of top right rocker.

Tall, shaped rabbit ears accentuate the shapely carved headpiece of this rocker. Twelve spindles join the lower rail. The arms curve outward to compliment the round cane seat supported by five matching spindles. The legs and H-rungs are also turned for added beauty. $475

Top row, left to right:

Outstanding triple pressed rocker is elaborately decorated with intricate scrolled pressings. Seven diagonally-set, turned, fluted spindles join the lower decorated rail. Backposts are turned and fluted. The arms are supported by matching spindles. The original pressed seat displays a unicorn. The skirt is shaped and intricately pressed. Even the legs are tapered, turned, and fluted as they set upon the rockers—and are joined by turned rungs. $900

Slat-back rocker with deep molded veneer seat offers comfort with shaped arms supported by five spindles and larger armposts which continue to form the front legs. $450

Center row, left to right:

Tall, pressed back rocker has ten spindles joining the top and bottom rails. The tall rabbit ears are turned and fluted. The bent arms are supported by four matching spindles and a larger armpost which attaches to the side of the seat. A reinforcing rod holds the arm in place and a tension rod secures the armposts for extra durability. $500

Tall rocker shows decorative incised carving surrounding the finger-grip at the top of the headpiece. A center rail is shaped and trimmed with beads as the irregularly spaced spindles connect the lower decorated rail. The bent arms curve gently, surrounding the round cane seat. The wide-shaped skirt is decoratively pressed. $550

Center row, right top:

Spindled rocker is lightly incised on the shaped headpiece. Seven turned spindles connect the lower rail with ball trimmings. An additional rail adds strength. The shapely arms are supported by turned posts which also form the front legs. The boxed seat adds strength and support for the upholstered spring seat. $675

Center row, right bottom:

Matched pair of elm rockers. Double broad panels display lightly embossed large pressings. Full curl bent arms are securely bolted to the seat and supported by three turned spindles. The owners have said they will rock into old age together in this great pair. $1,500 pair.

Bottom row, left to right:

Purely plain Mission-style rocker, identified by its straight lined construction and style. Undecorated, with newly upholstered spring seat. $375

Wicked Northwind appears in this rocker's crest supported by long intricately turned spindles. The round cane seat sets deeply within the shapely arms supported by long spindles and larger armpost. The seat is contoured to follow the roundness of the caning. The legs are turned, as are all the rungs. $750

Right:

Tall Bentwood arrowback rocker with broad, deeply carved headpiece. The full curl bentwood arms are bolted securely to the backposts and to the solid sculptured seat. Design makes this rocker most comfortable. $650

Left: Triple pressed rocker has turned backposts, 7 spindles, bent arms and cane seats. **Right:** Beautifully carved spindled rocker with molded veneer seat. Shaped arms are supported by diagonal turned spindles. The heavier front arm support also forms the leg attached to the side of the seat. The larger diagonal back arm support also forms the leg which comes to a vertical angle for strength when rocked. The legs are further reinforced with a turned front rung and side rungs which support the long arm spindles. $550

Top row, left to right:
Elm rocker with large floral carvings decorating the crest. Eight long turned spindles join the shaped saddle seat. Full curl bent arms are supported by three turned spindles. $600

Vibrantly grained, this solid quartered oak rocker is decoratively carved on its round back with a shaped and pressed center panel. The solid seat is softly contoured, the legs are shaped with clawfeet. The legs are further trimmed with corner braces which soften the abrupt lines as they meet the seat. $475

Simply designed with curved headpiece, long turned spindles to the solid sculptured seat and shaped arms. $375

Early chestnut rocker is unadorned, however stately. The broad headpiece is supported by a large, shaped center back panel with a single arrowback spindle to each side. The bentwood arms, supported by three spindles, flow from the headpiece, shape the arm, and curl to meet the solid seat. The legs and rungs are turned. $600

Center row, left to right:
Solid quartered oak slat back chairs. The straight lines are softened by the curved crest, shaped arms and legs, The boxed construction supports the upholstered seat. Not fancy, but comfortable. $450

Pressed back rocker has wide pressed headpiece, long turned spindles to the solid dished seat. The arms are shaped and supported by six straight spindles and a larger, turned armpost. $450

Mission style solid quartered oak rocker shows off its vibrant grain as its only decoration. $400

Bottom row, left to right:
Beautiful quadruple-pressed rocker shows intricate designs on the headpiece, pierced center back panel, lower rail, and a bit on the skirt. The sideposts are turned and reeded. The bent arms are supported by four turned spindles and larger armpost with a strengthening rod under the cane seat. $600

Unusual rocker with newly upholstered back and seat. The rounded arms are supported by eight turned spindles. They bow forward as if to welcome you to sit. $800

Elaborately decorated lady's sewing rocker with a deeply embossed headpiece and center back panel. The center and lower rails, along with the shaped skirt, add flair with a bit of carving. The one piece backpost legs are turned as are the front legs and rungs. $400

Panel back rocker has a broad, shaped headpiece supported by two turned spindles to each side of a wide shaped center panel. The embossed fiber-board seat is deep with shaped arms, supported by five turned spindles and armpost. The seat is skirted, adding depth with turned legs and rungs. $650

Top row, left to right:
Triple pressed high back rocker with decorated double lower rails, broad quartered headpiece, seven spiral spindles and double decorated lower rails. Bent arms are supported by four turned spindles and larger armpost joined below the seat with strengthening rod. $700

Plain, shaped slat back rocker with deep cane seat. The shaped arms are supported by six tapered spindles. The larger, turned armpost forms the legs. It is securely fastened as it meets the seat. $500

Eastlake style rocker, characterized by its straight outline and incised center panel with two straight slats to each side. The backposts form curled finials. The arms, square cut, are straight with rounded ends decorated on the lower side with scallops to meet the spindles. $475

Center row, left to right:
Delicately designed spindled rocker has carved crest between tall finials. The eleven long, tapered spindles are spaced with oak beads above as trim. The cane seat is square cut and the arms are unusually short. $450

Tall, double-pressed rocker has both center back panel and spindles. The shapely headpiece is horizontally pressed above a wheat pattern, embossed on the center panel above the second rail. Straight spindles connect the mid and lower rails. The arms are plain, but shaped with one armpost. The seat is upholstered with a round pad. The legs and rungs are plain. $600

Intricately spindled triple pressed rocker. The high-curved headpiece connects the middle rail with short stick 'n ball spindles which is then joined to the lower rail by ten intricately turned, long spindles. The arms are flat but curved and joined to the armpost, leg, and the rear leg by larger Stick 'n ball spindlework. The cane seat is square with simply pressed skirt. $450

High back, double-pressed rocker. The shaped double back exhibits fancy embossing with long, turned spindles joining the deep cane seat. The shaped arms are supported by four long, turned spindles. The legs and rungs are turned. $500

Bottom row, left to right:
The rocker with rectangular headpiece is softened by three shaped slats bearing carved decoration. Square arms are slightly curved and supported by a square cut armpost and leg. The solid seat is contoured for comfort. The legs are reinforced with wide face board. $450

Steam bent, quarter-sawn veneer rocker displays vivid grain as it curves and rolls to form a comfortable deep seat. Shaped arms are supported by the legposts and reinforced with horizontal braces with arrowback slats. $500

Double carved rocker displays beautifully turned spindles and sideposts. The armposts are curved, supporting the arms and surrounding the round caned seat. $650

Left:
Triple pressed rocker sits tall with its elaborately decorated headpiece showing center quarter grain. Eleven intricately turned spindles connect the decorated middle rail as the lower rail reverses the middle rail's design. Bentwood arms are supported by four turned spindles and larger turned armposts. The shaped cane seat curves for comfort with a shaped skirt framed by turned legs and rungs. $700

Right:
Simply designed panelback rocker displays vivid quarter-sawn grain. The arms are gracefully curved with turned posts, legs, and rungs. $400

Intricately spindled carved rocker, a wonderful design. The incised headpiece sits between large, turned single post back legs with distinctive, shaped and fluted finials. The lower carved rail and curved arms are supported by many intricately turned spindles. The face of the arms and box seat are also carved to enhance the needlepoint upholstered spring seat. $1,200

Left:
Panelback, late Mission style, solid-seated rocker is decorated by rope-twisted sideposts, arm supports and rope-twisted legs. $400

Right:
Undecorated rocker displays quarter grain oak on its center back panel. Large, double spindles support the curved, rounded arms. $400

Outstanding rocker has a beautifully decorated, broad back with carvings to accentuate the vibrant quarter grain framed in the round. The deep, wide seat rolls to an ornamental carved front. The high shaped arms are attached to the seat by five fancy, turned spindles and continuous shaped front posts. The small, lower panel is reinforced with seven short-turned spindles. $900

This sewing rocker is plain in its style, with a faint pressing set between shaped finials. Six straight spindles join the lower rail. The legs are turned under the seat with a single turned rung. $225

Quadruple pressed panel back rocker is intricately decorated. Bent arms are supported by four turned spindles and larger side mounted armposts with a strengthening dowel connecting the two beneath the seat. $675

COFFEE TABLES

Quartered oak radiates on the 18" tea table. The top rests on a turned column and shaped legs extend from the base. (24" diameter, 18" high), $750.

Once serving as a library table, these legs have been shortened to create a massive coffee table. The top (28" x 48") has rounded corners, a shelf for magazines and two drawers for storage. It is a most useful adaption. $800

Four columns support the round, quarter-sawn top of this coffee table. The columns rest on a platform shelf above curled feet. $700

Bent hickory legs support the oak top of this coffee table as a smaller round shelf rests on dowels joining the legs. Signed "Old Hickory, Martinsdale, Indiana." (30" diameter, 18" high), $650.

Originally a filing cabinet, this piece now serves as a coffee table. Deeply cut, square, raised panels decorate the back and sides while the face displays nine drawers with original brass pulls and hardware. Bun feet were added. $1,200

This oval coffee table (28" x 45") has a solid, quarter-sawn top on double pedestals. The platform rests on curled feet set diagonally. $900

Turned legs joined by shaped stretchers support the rectangular top of this coffee table. $450

Double pedestals stand on a platform base to support the solid, quartered, oval top (24" x 38") of this coffee table. The platform curves inward to meet curled feet extending on each side. A straight apron conceals a drawer. $700

Elegantly styled, this elongated (30" x 48") oval tea table has a solid, quarter-sawn top with rounded edges above a beaded apron. The shaped shelf joins end panels which flow into graceful, curled feet. $1,250

SETTEES

Lion-headed serpents create an undulating outline as their tails curl to meet the turned back posts. Thirteen intricate spindles support the back and shaped arms, with their spindles curving to frame the sculptured seat. Turned legs, with double rungs and stretchers, support this elaborate settee. $1,900

The pressed/carved image of legendary Northwind stands above the rail and numerous spindles shaping the back and arms of this settee. $1,800

Applied scroll carvings decorate the back of this settee above upholstered back rests and seat. A matching armchair is not shown. $450 set.

Three shaped and pierced splats form the back of this settee with spindles supporting shaped arms which extend from turned backposts. The quarter-sawn seat is sculptured for two or three occupants. It rests on turned legs with turned rungs and double stretchers. The settee is shown with its matching armchair. $1,800 set.

The carved "Northwind" face looks on as the focal point from the center back of this petite settee and matching arm and side chair. The ribband-back stands 34" tall as the stick'n ball spindles frame the masque and decorate the curved arms encircling the upholstered seat. Cabriole legs curve delicately to the floor, resting on porcelain castors. 42" wide and 21" deep, seating for two is provided.

The complimentary arm chair stands 31½" tall and 24" wide with a 20" deep seat. The side chair is smaller at 17½" wide x 16½" deep at the seat, with upholstered back a mere 29" tall. $2,400 parlor set.

PARLOUR TABLES

Top row, left to right:
The shaped, solid quartered oak top and apron of this table are supported by tapered legs joined by a scalloped shelf. The brass handle is on what appears to be a drawer, but is actually a pull-out writing surface. $750

The rounded edge of this solid quartered parlor table shades a ram's head carving at the center of the apron on each side. Cabriole legs are joined by a shaped shelf. $400

Center row, left to right:
The 28"-square, solid quartered oak top of this parlor table rests on turned legs with large, glass ball and claw feet. A square shelf joins the legs. $500

The square top of this parlor table is decorated with a pressed apron. Turned legs on small, glass ball and claw feet are joined by a shaped shelf. $400

Beautifully turned and rope-twisted legs support the round, solid quartered-oak top of this large parlor table with a shaped shelf joining the legs. $800

Bottom row, left to right:
Four, open-mouthed, griffin heads protrude inward from turned legs to support the lower shelf of this otherwise-unadorned parlor table. $475

Solid, quartered oak forms the top of this parlor table with a shaped, veneered apron. Turned, tapered, and twisted legs are joined by a shaped shelf. $375

Left:
The solid, quartered-oak, double round top of this parlor table is supported by four columns mounted on a platform base. Feet extend from beneath the platform to balance the table. $600

Right:
The round top of this parlor table rests on a center pedestal and four shaped legs. $400

This parlor table has a shaped top and serpentined apron. The curving legs meet a four-leaf-clover-shaped shelf. $450

The solid, quartered oak, oval top of this parlor table has a shaped edge on legs which curve inward to meet a shaped shelf. $450

Top row, left to right:
The round top of this parlor table is supported by spool-turned legs joined and strengthened by a small, square shelf. $225

Simply serviceable, this 24"-square parlor table has no apron and sparsely turned legs joined by a square shelf. $200

A shaped top and curved legs create grace in this un-decorated parlor table. $175

Center row, left to right:
This shaped parlor table has a solid, quartersawn oak top with beveled edge. Cabriole legs extend from the corners of the scalloped, serpentined apron inwardly meeting the shaped shelf and resting on carved, claw feet. $450

Solid quartered oak is featured in this set of four nested tables. Straight, tapered legs support each table which are 3¼" smaller and 1½" shorter than the previous ones as they decrease in size. The largest is 24⅝" wide x 14¾" deep x 30" high. The smallest is 15" wide x 14¾" deep x 25½" high. $600 set.

Bottom row, left to right:
An unusually shaped, solid quarter-sawn top on this parlor table rests on a round apron and tightly spooled, tapering legs. $375

The oval top this parlor table rests on a rectangular boxed frame and spiral-twisted legs are set in the corners as square and again at the floor as stretchers join the legs to each other. $225

"Stick 'n ball" turnings decorate the corners of this parlor table. Spindled railings decorate a large shelf where the square, grooved legs meet it, then taper and flair. $550

Fancy, turned legs support the solid, quartered oak double top of this parlor table. $275

The round top on this parlor table is supported by a shaped pedestal and a platform base. $450

Double round shelves with beveled edges are supported by triple columns on this solid, quartersawn oak parlor table as they rest on a tripod, claw-footed base. The table was made in Boston, Mass. $600

Graceful legs flow upward and fold inward to their sawtooth decoration as they support the shaped top of this parlor table. Collection of Lisa and Robert Stull.

Top row, left to right:
Cabriole legs support the 24"-round, solid, quartered oak top of this graceful parlor table. $400

Solid, quartered oak was chosen for this rectangular, 24"-wide x 16"-long, parlor table. A drawer is provided as the straight tapered legs are reinforced by a shaped shelf. $375

The most irregularly shaped top of this parlor table rests on large, turned spindles standing on the corners of its shaped shelf. Small cabriole legs curve to the floor. $450

Center row, left to right:
Turned legs decorate this small parlor table with a beveled-edge top. An oak bead attaches the shelf to the splayed legs. $150

Quartered oak is on the round top of this parlor table with turned legs joined by a square shelf. $375

Scroll carved ends distinctively decorate this solid, quarter-sawn oak parlor table as they support the shaped top and two shelves. Notice the lower shelf which extends beyond the curve of the legs. $500

Bottom row, left to right:
Art Nouveau style is evident on this solid, quarter-sawn oak parlor table in the graceful, U-shaped support joining the top to the base by a shelf which rests on straight, yet shaped, legs. $400

Beautiful, solid quartered oak is in the top of this softly contoured parlor table. The curves are defined by a deeply cut edge. The shaped apron, cabriole legs, and shaped shelf add to its graceful lines. $450

Solid, quartered oak creates the top of this parlor table. Turned legs with glass ball and claw feet are joined by a shaped shelf. $400

PARLOR DESKS

Top row, left to right:
A grotesque mask and applied scroll carvings decorate the drop front of this parlor desk with four storage drawers. $1,275

Solid, quartered oak enhances the straight lines of this Mission style parlor desk. $900

Three double-swelled drawers and shaped legs ornament an otherwise undecorated parlor desk. $800

Bottom row, left to right:
The central, applied carving accents the drop front of this parlor desk. Shaped edges create an interesting outline. $1,000

Vividly grained, quartered oak veneer radiates on the drop front and three serpentined drawers of this parlor desk. $1,200

Brass strap hinges and large drawer pulls ornament the drop front of this parlor desk. Scroll carvings decorate the arched crest and corners of the lid. $1,200

Beautifully designed and decorated, this French style parlor desk has delicate scroll carvings accentuating the curves and brass filigree mounts on the knees of cabriole legs. The stepped-down interior forms an arch. $1,500

Solid quarter-sawn oak and carved lower corners lower decorate the drop front of this elegant parlor desk. Two drawers bow slightly to meet cabriole legs with incised knees. The interior as pigeon holes and two small, bowed drawers. $1,400

Advertised as the "Lady Washington Boudoir Desk No. 15" in the 1908 Larkin catalog, this desk was exchanged for five Larkin certificates or $10.00 worth of Larkin products. Select, quarter-sawn oak and scroll carvings accent the beveled mirror, drop front, and skirt. French legs support the desk. $900

Top row, left to right:
A large, beveled mirror rests above sloping side panels and a scroll-carved, drop front on this French style parlor desk. Cabriole legs are adorned with brass mounts on the knees and tips of the front legs. $1,275

Solid, quartered oak is set diagonally on the drop front of this parlor desk. Brass spindle railings ornament the shelf and serpentined drawers protrude to meet side posts which join cabriole legs with satyr-masques at the knees. $1,200

Center row, left to right:
Delicate scroll carvings decorate the drop front of this parlor desk. Serpentine drawers have fancy brass pulls and the carved skirt curves to join carved knees on legs which taper to claw feet. $1,350

Plain and simple, this parlor desk has a shaped, beveled mirror with carved crest. $700

Bottom row, left to right:
Deeply cut scrolls decorate the drop front of this parlor desk with double drawers and shaped legs. $1,050

Carved corners accentuate the drop front of this parlor desk with a shaped beveled mirror. A single drawer and carved double doors enclosing the storage shelf below. $950

A solitary, applied carving ornaments the center drop front of this small, straight-sawn parlor desk. A scalloped edge to the single drawer, slightly curved legs, and shaped shelf add beauty. $450

Left:
Select, quarter-sawn veneer applied in a pattern of this parlor desk is enhanced by thin, deeply curved front legs. $700

Right:
Shaped legs and fancy brass drawer pulls ornament this otherwise plain parlor desk. $650

Left and below:
Solid, quarter-sawn oak is on the drop front of this undecorated parlor desk. Straight legs are joined by a shelf. The desk is fitted with a nice interior. $675

Left:
Two textured glass doors enclose a storage area molding of this elaborate desk. A carved masque and scrolls decorate the flush, drop front of the center desk and carved panels flank the doors. Pulls for the two drawers appear as mustachioed faces and winged serpents form corner braces. $2,800

Top row, left to right:
Curio cabinets with bowed glass doors flank an oval mirror above the decorated drop front desk. Drawers below the desk rest on legs joined by shelves detailed with delicate turned spindles. This fancy parlor desk remains in its immaculate, original finish. $3,500

Darkened and dirty, this drop front desk shows potential beauty. The shapely outline, incised carving, and beveled mirror will shine once a new finish is applied. $900 refinished.

Incised carvings, an irregular outline at the crest, a curio shelf, bowed door, shapely mirror, and a bowed drawer add interesting character to this side-by-side desk. $1,900

Center row, left to right:
Graceful legs support this drop-front desk. The straight lines of the top are softened by the slightly serpentined drawer with its center carving. The scalloped side panels and drawer face add graceful touches to its style. $1,000

This beautiful double, side by side desk with its bookcases flanking the drop front desk and storage drawers is now used as a cruio. It displays prized items as well as its immaculate original finish. $2,300

Bottom row, left to right:
Unusually divided, this side by side desk offers a narrow bookcase, enclosed by a bowed glass door. It now serves as a curio displaying its bird collection. The drop front desk is wider than usual, giving comfortable space to write. A closed storage area is provided below the desk, along with a mirrored curio shelf and enclosed what-not box above. A kitchen shelf clock is displayed on the top, along with several pieces of blue delft. A most inviting area to write a note to a friend as a rose awaits the use of its space. $2,000

Most elegant in its style, this beautiful secretary desk stands 83" high. The face of the 40" wide by 18½" deep, drop front desk displays outstanding carvings on its framed center panel. A deeply carved shell is the focal point as it is flanked by swirled, foliated patterns to each side. The carving continues on the face of the pantry door below. A shapely, carved skirt adds the finishing touch above the floor. Notice the three drawers and the bookcase top bear no adornment, but serve to enhance the carved areas. Entirely of solid quartersawn oak, this example is exquisite. An oak piano stool stands nearby. $3,200

English Chippendale styling is evident in this blick front desk that is entirely of grain matched, selected, solid quartersawn oak. Outstanding in tis casual formality, this desk reflects superior quality and elegance.

Each block drawer face is constructed in three pieces. The center panel is shaped to form the undulating design with the ends mounted to overlap the center panel, forming the recess, adding the dimension, and providing a flat area for the period style drawer pulls.

The drawer face is dovetailed into the drawer sides, which are equipped with glides along the lower edge to guide the drawer as it slide into the case.

Each side is a continuous flow of fine quartersawn grain patterns. The edges at the front are rounded, meeting the graceful bracketed ball-and-claw feet at the floor. The side meets the back in a more defined curve. Actually, the back leg is the extension of a vertical member, shaping the curve the entire height of the desk as it curves around the corner to meet the railing across the top. A very close look can reveal the joining. The entire back is enclosed and finished.

This desk is fitted with a most elegant interior. The six small, dovetailed drawers flow with shaped faces from slightly concave to convex, following the shapely lines of the framing. Notice the detailed shape of the cubby dividers and their valance. Two brass arms give strong support, allowing the writing surface to rest slightly below level. This feature enhances comfort as the surface slants slightly toward the writer. What a pleasure to absorb the beauty and workmanship found in this superior desk. $2900

ROMAN CHAIRS

Top row, left to right:
Outstanding Roman chair with wide pierced back and Northwind blowing. Three-dimensional Cherubic faces adorn the backposts flowing into shapely arms. The X-shaped construction is carved on the front panels and decorated with another Cherubic face. The legs end in lion's paw feet. $950

Handsome Roman chair with shaped quartersawn back decorated with applied carvings and Northwind face. The seat is deep with curved arms. $650

Center row, left to right:
Impressive high-grade Roman chair with tall, heavily carved back which flows into broad arms ending in full-dimensional lion heads. The recently upholstered seat sits in the curve of the crossing legs and the intersection is faced with a carved medallion. The legs have clawfeet and are joined front to back by bold turned stretchers. $1,100

The original patina glows on this beautiful original finish Roman chair. The carved, shaped back has a horned masque surrounded with scrolls. The tall backpost are carved lion heads. The quartered oak grain shines on the concave seat, decorated on the face with a center shell design. The curved legs have clawfeet. $750

Bottom row, left to right:
Vivid quartered oak grain is displayed on the broad back of this massive Roman chair. Side posts display open-mounted lion heads. The shaped arms are set high above the curved quartersawn seat supported by square carved spindles. The arm and seat facings are trimmed with applied scrolls. The legs have heavy clawfeet. $800

An outrageously carved, grotesque mask dominates the back panel of this Roman chair. The shaped arms and vibrantly quarter grained seat add to its style with turned rungs connecting the legs. A partial paper label reveals its origin to be Grand Rapids, Michigan. Collection of Lisa and Robert Stull. $800

Conservatively decorated Roman chair show vibrant quarter grain on the back panel, seat, and face of the curved legs. Scrolled carving accents the backposts. $475

Dining Room

CLAW PEDESTAL TABLES

America dined well in the 1880s during a time of comfortable prosperity. Although the average worker earned well under $1000 annually, food was plentiful and the cost of it in 1882 remained the same as it had been 40 years before.

How food was served and the surroundings of its consumption became important to the householders and good business for the manufacturers of china, silver, and furniture.

The arbiters of good taste at that time possessed conflicting ideas about decor, but they all agreed that the dining room probably was the most important room in the house. One designer noted that if one sumptuous room could be afforded, it should be the dining room.

Dining rooms were to the modest homes of the 1880s as family rooms are today. A day bed in the corner was not unusual. A clock would have rested upon its wall shelf and a heating stove would be found, too.

The square or round extension table dominated the room as it was almost always placed in the center under a pull-down kerosene lamp. The basic pieces of a well-furnished dining room also included dining chairs with taller host and hostess chairs, a sideboard, a buffet with glass doors, and a carving table or dinner wagon.

By 1890, most dining suits were shown in oak or mahogany. Sideboards and china closets were mounted on high legs so that a "broom would readily reach beneath them." Buffet tops were low and usually had a plate glass mirror at the back under a single shelf. China cabinets showed off mirrored backs, glass shelves, and plate glass fronts and sides. Prices for these cabinets ranged from $30 to over $100 at the time.

This 44" diameter, pedestal, clawfoot dining table has petite lion heads carved on the knees. $1,600

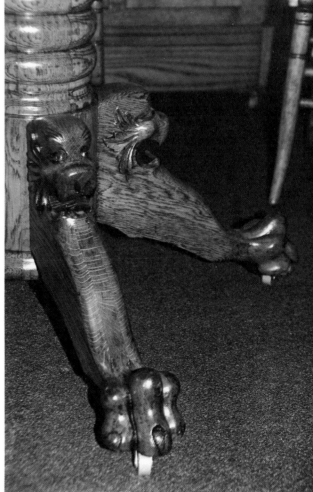

A 54" diameter, pedestal dining table has predominant, large-knuckled, five-toed carved, claw feet and two extending leaves. $2,250

An elegant, 48" diameter, solid quarter-sawn, pedestal dining table with a sculptured apron and high, shaped knees which slope gracefully into carve claw feet. The top opens with five extending leaves. $1,800

A distinctive, split-pedestal dining table with a solid, quarter-sawn, 54" diameter top with shaped and decorated apron. The large pedestal is shaped and fluted with low, sloping, carved knees and claw feet with three carved toes and spurs. $2,250

This 42" diameter, straight-sawn, plain pedestal, dining table has low graceful legs with claw feet. $1,350

Large, carved lion heads decorate the pedestal of the 48"
diameter, carved, solid quartered oak dining table. The
lions, with fanged mouths open, peer over high-knuckled
and spurred claw feet. $3,200

A massive, claw-footed platform, with split-pedestal, supports this 54" diameter, solid quartered oak dining table.
The claws are accentuated with scrolls and feathers to soften
the junction between the platform and the clawfeet. The
top opens with five extension leaves. $2,400

Graceful, softly rounded, claw-footed legs reach out from
the turned pedestal of this beautiful, grained-matched dining table. The beveled edge sets off the sculptured apron
of the 48" diameter top. $2,500

A divided platform pedestal and center pillar support this elegant 50" wide x 60" long oval table top. Its vividly quarter-cut striped oak apron and unusual style of clawfeet make it an unusual example. $2,500

Vividly grained quartered veneer highlights this 48" diameter, clawfoot, pedestal dining table with three 9" wide extension leaves. $1,500

A tapered, fluted pedestal enhances this 44" diameter, quartered veneer dining table. The three leaves are straight-sawn as is often the case when they are later additions to the table, as these are. Matching grain was not of concern since usually the leaves are covered by a table cloth when they are being used. $1,400

Simply styled, this 42" wide, solid quartered dining table with shaped apron, split-pedestal, and square-cut, claw-footed legs opens to accommodate three quarter-sawn leaves. $1,600

This vibrant, 45" diameter, split pedestal, claw-footed dining table with a tiger-striped, veneered top and pedestal radiates as it sets in the sun. Two 12" leaves are straight sawn. $1,800

This highly figured, 54" diameter, solid quartered table top has rounded edge and a sculptured band. It is outstanding with a massive, claw-footed, split-pedestal platform base and large scrolls. Its extension capacity accommodates more than the three, 9" wide leaves. $2,600

Massive claw legs curve from the split pedestal of this 54" diameter, solid quartered dining table. Eight, 12" wide, quartered leaves rest on slides to expand the top to a 12'6" long, elongated oval. $2,800

The outstanding, solid, quartered oak, 54" diameter dining table is complemented by its deeply sculptured band, ornately scrolled legs, and high-knuckled, detailed, claw feet which extend from a split pedestal. Four leaves rest on the extending slides. $3,500

Talon claws and ball feet adorn the rounded feather-carved legs of this 54" diameter, pedestal table. Five 8" wide leaves rest on the extended slides. $2,500

The 48" diameter, claw-footed dining table displays beautiful decoration on its turned and fluted pedestal with high, curved and carved knees which slope into detailed, high-knuckled and spurred claw feet. The veneered top opens to take three extensions leaves. $2,400

Wonderfully supported by four movable claw-footed columns along with a center solid pillar, this 48" diameter, solid quartered dining table opens and closes distinctively to take its three 12" long leaves. $2,600

Absolutely stunning, this 60" diameter, solid quartered-oak dining table displays a beautiful grain-matched top and sculptured band above a carved split pedestal. The platform base is most unusual with upside down carved claws with toenails gripping the underside of the platform. Seven, 9" wide, quartersawn leaves extend this table to double its closed size. $3,500

High-knuckled, spurred claw feet decorated the turned and fluted pedestal of this 42" diameter dining table. The straight-grained top opens to receive two 10" wide leaves. $1,500

Open-mouthed lions with their tongues protruding decorate the knees and carved base of this 54" diameter claw footed pedestal table. Flattened knuckles and wide toes sit squarely on the floor. Four 10" wide leaves expand the top. $3,000

This octagon-shaped pedestal has lion heads and scrolls curling outward above its claw feet, supporting the 54" diameter top. $2,600

Right:
An elegant, 48" diameter, solid quartered oak dining table has a beveled edge, sculptured apron, and turned and fluted pedestal. Shaped legs, which are defined by a routed line contouring the knees ending in claw feet. $1,800

This elegant, talon-claw and ball-footed pedestal dining table accents its 48" diameter, solid, quartered-oak top with a gadrooned edge and vividly grained apron. The shaped pedestal has fluted trim above and below the rounded legs. $3,700

Quartered oak veneer covers the top and apron of this 42" diameter, pedestal table. Simply designed, the straight center pedestal rest on its platform base supported by carved claw feet. $1,200

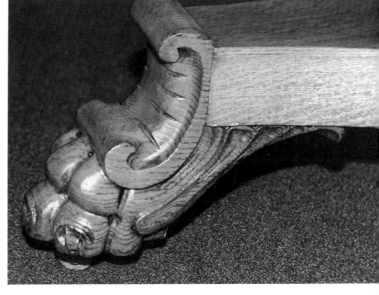

Outstanding solid quartered oak 54" square dining table with a shaped band rest upon a large platform pedestal. The beaded trim adds detail. The scrolled, claw feet gracefully support the table. $2,500

ANIMAL TABLES

Three large, carved griffins sit upon the carved platform base of this ornate center hall table. Their bodies support the 48"-diameter, quartersawn top which displays an elaborately carved border and gadrooned edge. $6,000

The elaborately carved pedestal of this 60" diameter, carved top dining table extends its legs in the shape of winged dogs resembling Scotland terriers. Truly unique in its design. $8,500

Four full-bodied, winged griffins dominate the base of this 60" -diameter dining table as they crouch on claw-footed platforms around the huge center pillar. The scroll-carved apron and gadrooned top create an outstanding table, in its original finish. $12,000

Center left and bottom left photographs are details of table on opposite page bottom.

NON-CLAW TABLES

An intricately decorated cast iron base supports the 36"
diameter, round, quartered oak top of this pedestal table.
Designed to be bolted to the floor, it originally was used in
the club car of a train. $750

A tapered, grooved, square pedestal with rope-twist trim
rests on a shaped platform with contoured feet. $1,400

Open graining is displayed well on this 42" diameter, round
dining table with three leaves. A double turned pedestal is
supported by shaped but plain legs. $750

Vibrant, solid quartered-oak forms the 54" diameter, round top of this dining table. The massive split pedestal is octagonal with large scrolled legs which curl upward at the ends. Quartered-oak veneer covers the legs. $1,800

Tiger-grained oak is brilliant on this 48" diameter dining table. The veneer was applied in a vivid pattern. The large, center pillar rests on a round platform supported by wide, squared, curled legs. $1,200

Turned-up feet with sloping legs are mounted on the ribbed pedestal of this 42" diameter dining table top. $1,000

Veneered quartered oak shines with highlights on the top of this 48" diameter, dining table. The octagonal pedestal rests on a platform with curled legs extending from the corners. $1,200

DINING CHAIRS

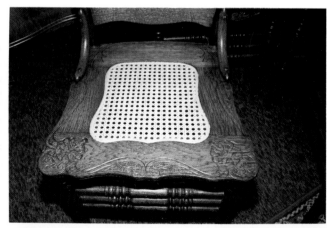

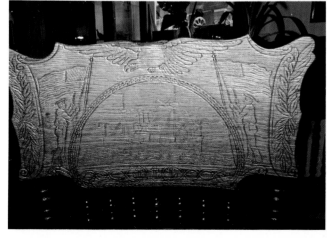

Elaborately decorated "Maine" pressedbacks are quadruple pressed with a military motif. They are embossed with the *Battleship Maine* on the broad headpiece commemorating the Spanish-American War victory of 1898. The sideposts are turned and spiraled as are the seven spindles. The seat is shaped and pressed above the pressed skirt. Turned rungs strengthen the tapered legs. $1800 set of four.

Handsome set of six panelback dining chairs have pressed cane seats. The legs slightly curve, adding to their quiet style. $1,250 set.

Tall pair of bentwood arrowback dining chairs. Shaped slats add to their comfort. The sideposts are distinctively turned with finials to frame the carved headpiece. $600 pair.

Pair of Queen Anne style side chairs are curvaceously shaped with deeply bowed knees and large, carved claw feet. $850 pair.

Set of four double pressed dining chairs. The headpiece displays a musical lyre. "Milk bottle" finials, turned sideposts, and seven spindles enhance the design. $1,200 set.

Top row, left to right:
This set of four Barroom or Captain's chairs (1850-1870) are comfortable with their rounded backs supported by eight turned spindles. The arms are a continuation of the back as they come around the chair and bend to the star-patterned perforated seat. $750 set.

This pair of triple-pressed dining chairs has three separate back panels, with the second and third joined by seven straight spindles. $450 pair.

This dining chair has a wide headpiece with an elaborate feather press design. Intricately turned and decorated sideposts frame the seven turned spindles joining the lower rail. The skirt is also pressed above three turned rungs and shaped legs. $225 single.

Ornately carved and upholstered set of four includes two armchairs and two sidechairs. The tall, carved back is scrolled with large turnings to each side of the back rest. The arms have grotesque heads on each end, supported by large, turned spindles. The legs, rungs, and stretchers are also elaborately turned. $4,000 set.

Center row, left to right:
The fierce "Northwind" decorates the headpiece of this dining chair. Seven long, turned spindles join the lower decorated rail set between turned and fluted one-piece back post legs. $1,250 set of four.

Set of six "Vienna diners" or Ice Cream Parlor chairs. The double hoop bentwood backs bend and flow to form the back legs. The round quartersawn ply seats rest on the bent legs which are reinforced by a bentwood ring joining the legs along the inside. "Hiphuggers," or braces, reinforce the hoop back to the seat. $900 set.

Turned backposts enhance the simple style of this set of five panelback dining chairs. Turned legs and triple-turned rungs are the only other detail. $900 set of four.

The pierced center panel of this dining chair sets between the lower curves of the headpiece. This set of four is simply in style. $1,200 set.

Bottom row, left to right:
Elaborately decorated, this set of six quadruple-pressed panelback dining chairs have tall turned finials and fluted backposts framing the three upper decorated panels. The pressed skirt sets between turned, flared legs above triple turned rungs. $2,100 set.

The pierced center panel takes the eye on this set of six elegant dining chairs. Set between flowing back legs, the center panel broadens into the crest as it rolls into a scroll. $1,400 set.

Kissing dolphins adorn the headpiece of this set of five dining chairs. Seven spindles joined the decorated lower rail set between turned, tapered, and fluted backposts. Turned legs and rungs add to the detailing. $1,100 set.

Set of six arrowback kitchen chairs. The flat slats and dipped seats are comfortable. The solid seats are reinforced for the prevention of splitting. Stamped *Wisler & Son, Philadelphia Paten 10/4/1898.* $1,100 set.

Top row, left to right:
In 1908, this Sears kitchen chair sold for $1.37 each. However inexpensive, it features a pressed headpiece (constructed of several plys), seven turned spindles, securely braced one piece backpost legs, a caned seat, turned legs and rungs—even a small skirt. These features are also found on more expensive chairs. $900 set of four.

Tall, elegantly decorated, triple pressed dining chair. The headpiece is artfully shaped. The backposts are turned, shaped and fluted. The seat is contoured above turned, tapered legs and triple turned rungs. $325 single.

Elegant set of six dining chairs with a carved and pierced center back panel. Thin, shapely arms attached to the boxed frame of the upholstered seat. The tapered legs rest on carved clawfeet. $1,800 set.

Set of four solid-seated pressedbacks have decorated headpieces set between tall finials with turned backposts. Five turned spindles support the crest. Turned legs and wide set turned rungs add detail. $1,200 set.

Center row, left to right:
The shapely, pressed headpiece, fluted finials, and small turned spindles decorate this single chair to be used with a desk. $175 single.

Beautifully "heart pressed" set of six dining chairs. The broad headpiece is intricately pressed set above seven turned spindles with turned, shaped, and fluted backposts. $2,400 set.

Finely detailed, this outstanding set of five quadruple-pressed panelback dining chairs displays its quartered grain within the beaded cameo of its headpiece. $2,000 set.

Bottom row, left to right:
Tremendous, intricately-pressed dining chairs. The broad headpiece and lower rail are elegantly shaped, connected by nine spiral spindles. The backpost legs are turned, shaped, and fluted as they frame the chair back. The rounded cane seat sets above turned, flared legs joined by triple turned rungs. $2,500 set of 6

This stylish and sturdy set of six, including one armchair, are completely constructed of solid quartered oak. The legs rest on carved clawfeet. $1,100 set.

Seven bent, turned spindles take the eye as they set between the decorated headpiece and lower rail of this single pressedback chair. Turned legs and rungs support the cane seat. $225 single.

The deeply embossed headpiece rests on turned and fluted backposts with seven turned spindles joining to the decorated lower rail. Turned legs and rungs add further interest. $250 single.

Scrolled pressings decorate the broad headpiece set between fluted finials. Seven turned spindles join the shaped lower rail. $800 set of three.

Simply designed set of four, the pierced center back panel adds interest as the crest flows to the corners and down the sides to form the legs. The quarter grain shines on the seat frame and the face of the fine legs. $1,200 set.

Top row, left to right:

Simply decorated set of four with touches of incised carving, the quarter grain radiates on the headpiece and broad lower rail. Six short tapered spindles join the two panels. $1,200 set.

Set of six ladderback dining chairs have a cut out headpiece, the lower portion of which duplicates the pattern of the second and third rails. The shaped, solid seat rests on turned legs with triple turned rungs. $1,800 set.

The faintly pressed headpiece of this single dining chair sets between tall, turned finials and backpost. Five long, turned spindles add support to the solid seat. $145 single.

Pair of Windsor-style hoopback armchairs with carved knuckles. The deeply sculptured solid seat makes this chair most comfortable. $750 pair.

Center row, left to right:

This single pressedback armchair has its decorated headpiece set between egg-shaped finials. Seven turned spindles connect to the lower rail. The bent arms curve from the backposts supported by four turned spindles and a larger turned armpost. Reinforcement rods hold the arm securely in place. $500

This set of six dining chairs display a shapely center back panel. The boxed frame provides support for the upholstered seat. Shaped legs rest on conservative clawfeet. $1,200 set.

The center pressing on this single armchair decorates the crest as it sets above six long, turned, and twisted spindles and between round finials. Bent arms flow from the backposts to curve into the armrests supported by four turned spindles and larger turned armpost. $550

This set of four double pressed dining chairs has turned finals and backpost with seven turned spindles joining the headpiece and lower rail. $1,200 set.

Bottom row, left to right:

This tall pair of triple pressed dining chairs displays an intricately decorated headpiece between tall shaped and fluted finials. Eight tapered twisted spindles join the lower decorated rail. Turned and fluted backpost legs flow to the floor. The caned seat is finished with a pressed skirt setting above three turned rungs. $900 pair.

This pair of tall slat back dining chairs displays a deeply carved headpiece, with turned backposts framing the shaped slats. $475 pair.

Elegant set of seven, including one armchair, displays a shapely, pierced center back panel and curved headpiece. $1,800 set.

Fierce Northwind shows his face on the crest of this comfortable ladderback chair. Graceful curves and shapely legs add to its style. $1,500 set.

Top row, left to right:
Stylish set of four, including one armchair, displays a pierced center back panel, a shapely crest and tapered clawfooted legs. $1,200 set.

This set of four dining chairs displays a wide scroll-pressed headpiece set between tall, tapered finials. Seven finely turned, short spindles join the broad lower rail. Tapered legs with turned rungs support the caned seat. $1,500 set.

The double pressings of this set of four dining chairs are enhanced by seven intricately turned spindles joining the headpiece and lower rail. The caned seat is skirted, framed by turned legs and rungs. $1,500 set.

Center row, left to right:
Set of five slat back, solid-seated, kitchen chair. The strong bentwood backposts support the crest along with five flat bent slats. This style is known as "Red Lion" chairs for their place of origin near York, Pennsylvania. $1,000 set.

This single maple, pressedback, dining chair displays a deeply embossed headpiece with seven turned and flattened spindles connecting the lower decorated rail. $175

This set of six intricately pressed dining chairs has a broad shaped headpiece decorated with flowers and scrolls. Turned, tapered, fluted backposts and seven turned and twisted spindles support the crest and connect the lower scroll-pressed rail. $2,500

Bottom row, left to right:
Quartered oak grain takes the center stage on the board headpiece of this set of four quadruple-pressed dining chairs. Delicate pressings trim the edges of the headpiece supported by turned, tapered and fluted backposts. Eight finely turned spindles join the lower rail as it is accented on the lower edge with fine embossing. The shaped cane seat is also pressed, as is the skirt above turned rungs joining double turned legs. $1,700 set of five.

This exceptional pair of double pressed armchairs displays a broad, intricately decorated headpiece. Eight rope-twisted spindles join the lower decorated rail. The backposts are turned and tapered as the bent arms flow into place, supported by four rope-twisted spindles and a larger turned armpost. Reinforcing rods hold the bent arm securely in place. The tapered legs are turned as are the triple rungs. $1,200 pair.

This sturdy set of four dining chairs displays a center carved crest mounted on heavy one-piece backpost legs. Thirteen straight spindles join the lower rail. The full boxed cane seat is supported by turned, tapered legs. $1,200 set.

Simply styled, this set of six dining chairs displays a deeply scroll-carved headpiece. Five long, turned spindles decorate the back between plain one-piece backpost legs. $1,500 set.

This set of six urn-shaped panelback dining chairs are unadorned except for the outstanding large, carved clawfooted legs. $1,200 set.

This tremendous set of six, 48" tall, arrowback armchairs is deeply carved across the crests, as if to crown the chairs. The bentwood arms roll to the seat supported by three turned spindles. The decorated skirt, tapered legs, and turned rugs add to their beauty. $4,500 set.

Cutouts and curves develop the character of this pair of dining chairs. The headpiece displays vivid quartered oak graining in its veneer. The fine legs taper gracefully to the floor. $450 pair.

Top row, left to right:
This pair of panelback armchairs displays a wide shaped center panel. The original black leather seats remain intact as they are supported by the boxed frame resting on shaped clawfooted legs. $650 pair.

This set of six dining chairs displays scroll pressings to the top and bottom of the center back upholstered panel. Shaped clawfooted legs support the caned seats. $1,800 set.

Beautifully ornamented, this set of six solid seated pressed-back dining chairs display an upward motion as the embossed pattern flows from the center to the outward corners of the headpiece. Turned sideposts and long, turned spindles to the seat enhance this set. $2,000 set.

Center row, left to right:
Solid quartered grain is displayed above a flower pressing on this set of four dining chairs. Turned and twisted backposts and seven turned and flattened spindles support the crest. $1,500 set of four.

This set of six dining chairs displays its quartered grain. Tall finials stand above the broad, undecorated headpiece joined to the lower rail by eight short spindles with ball trim across the bottom. $1,800 set of six.

This single maple dining chair is beautifully embossed. It is framed by tall beehive finials and turned back posts, and seven turned spindles join the solid seat. $250

Simply carved across the crest, the headpiece displays its quartered grain. Tall, tapered finials flow into single post back legs. Five turned spindles join the second rail. A third rail was added for additional strength. $1,200 set of four.

Bottom row, left to right:
Set of six dining chairs are unusually carved with figural designs on the center back panel. The seat is upholstered, resting on a boxed frame decorated on the face. The bulbous front legs are joined to the back legs by a single square stretcher. $1,800 set.

This curvaceous set of six dining chairs displays a shapely headpiece enhanced by the pierced center back panel. French-style legs support the caned seat. $1,600 set including 1 armchair.

This sturdy set of six Captain's chairs are exceptionally durable. The rounded back and sculptured seat provide comfort. The legs set squarely on the floor. The rear legs are set on a angle. As a person would rock back on this armchair, the rear legs move into the vertical position. This is the point of maximum strength, thus avoiding damage to the chair and, of course, its occupant. $1,200 set.

This set of four dining chairs is enhanced by the pierced center back panel displaying its quartered grain. Upholstered seats add comfort. The legs rest on carved clawfeet. $1,100 set.

Scrolled pressings handsomely decorates the crest and lower panel of this splat-back set of four dining chairs. $1,200 set.

This set of six displays a single pressing at the center crest. Seven turned spindles, a cane seat, and bamboo turned rungs add further style to the chair. $1,800 set.

A crescent pressing decorates the headpiece of this set of six dining chairs. Seven turned spindles join the decorated lower rail. The single post back legs wear tall, shaped finials with turnings and fluting. The legs are turned above and below the turned rungs. $1,800 set.

Top row, left to right:
This faintly-pressed single dining chair displays turned finials and sideposts. Four long, turned spindles join the headpiece to the solid seat. $175

Larkin armchairs. Two styles. The press is the same, however the spindles, lower press, armposts, rungs, and leg turnings are different. $750 each.

This large, single armchair displays a broad, scroll-pressed headpiece that rests upon eight turned spindles which connect to the lower decorated rail. The bentwood arms flow from the single post back and are supported by four turned spindles along with larger turned armposts. The large, caned seat is skirted with a tiny pressed rib. The turned legs are flared, joined by three turned rungs. $750

Center row, left to right:
This set of four dining chairs displays a lightly embossed pressing. Six beaded spindles dress up this set as do the cane seat, turned legs, and rungs. $1,000 set.

This beautiful set of six dining chairs displays an intricate flower and rope-twist pressing. The tall finials and turned and fluted backposts frame the double pressings and the seven turned spindles. The cane seat is skirted and supported by double turned legs and turned rungs. $2,400 set.

Simply decorated, this set of four kitchen chairs supports its scroll pressed headpiece with four long, turned spindles and turned sideposts connecting to the solid seat. $850 set.

Bottom row, left to right:
This tall set of six fan-back dining chairs display their shaped decorated headpiece supported by five long, turned spindles and turned sideposts mounted in the solid dished seat. Turned legs and triple turned rungs add to their style. $1,800 set.

This set of six solid seated, dining chairs displays a shaped top rail with five short spindles connecting a second high rail. Five long, turned spindles attach to the seat as do the heavier, turned sideposts. The braces are unusually long as they attach high on the post and anchor forward on the side of the seat for added strength to the back. $1,200 set.

Delicately pressed scrolls and beads decorate the headpiece of this set of five dining chairs. Six turned spindles support the crest as they join the lower rail which is decorated by a tiny rope-twist. The legs are turned under the caned seat, as are the rungs. $1,500 set.

The No. 11 "Larkin Pressedback" side chair is one of the most collectible of all the chair designs. Beautifully embossed on the headpiece and lower rail, they are accentuated by "milk bottle top" finials and turned and twisted single post back legs. Long, tapered spindles join the crest and lower rail above the shaped, caned and skirted seat. Turned legs and triple turned rungs support the chair. $375 each in sets.

Shown in the 1908 Larkin catalog, one side chair was given for one certificate and 25 cents. The matching armchair was available for two certificates. A set of six side chairs required seven certificates.

Collectors today accumulate large sets of these classic pressedbacks, as did the ladies of 1908. Sturdily constructed, they have come through the years to be restored and again serve their families. See opposite page top center.

Outstanding in style, this massive sideboard displays elaborate carvings everywhere! The richly ornamented, hooded top stands 7'8" high at its crest which protrudes above the large, domed, beveled mirror and carvings beneath. Lions spread their wings at the corners and rest on columns. Eight lion faces provide drawer pulls above and below carved doors in the 28"-deep x 72"-wide base. $10,000

Two oval, beveled mirrors flanking a larger, center, domed mirror above a full-width shelf. The 54"-wide base encloses silver and linen drawers with fancy brass pulls and gracefully decorated, raised panel cabinet doors. Small columns accent the shaped, fluted legs. $3,500

Open-mouthed, winged griffins sit on each side of the rectangular beveled mirror. Original dark varnish remains on the conservatively decorated base of this sideboard which rests on legs and claw feet. The maker's label reads, "Reaser Furniture Company, Gettysburg, Penna. Manufacturers." Courtesy of Lisa and Robert Stull. $1,800

Incised carvings decorate this Eastlake style sideboard. The straight lines are enhanced by a carved crest and turned spindles support the shelves. Off-set drawers are in the base cabinet. $2,500

The arched canopy top of this distinctive sideboard displays a carved, antlered deer head. Six small, beveled mirrors behind the shelves flank the large, center domed, beveled mirror. The detailed top rests on a base cabinet housing six drawers and three cabinets with carved doors. $12,000

Opposite page, bottom:
French-style and carved claw and ball feet enhance this "Larkin" buffet. Rounded ends and bowed glass curio doors frame the quartered oak center drawers. The elongated, oval, beveled mirror adds to the beauty. This design was shown as No. 220 in the 1912 Larkin catalog. Signed "Larkin Co., Buffalo, N.Y. Factory No. 18." $2,000

Beveled, glass-enclosed and mirror-backed cabinets stand on claw-footed supports above the massive base of this sideboard which rests on carved claw feet. $5,000

Tapered rope-twists support the wide, molded top of this large sideboard. Carved columns support the shelves and scroll-carved panels and beveled mirrors provide the background. "Northwind" faces, lion heads and grotesque cranes are carved into the drawers and doors of the massive base which retains its original finish. $4,500

BUFFETS/SERVERS

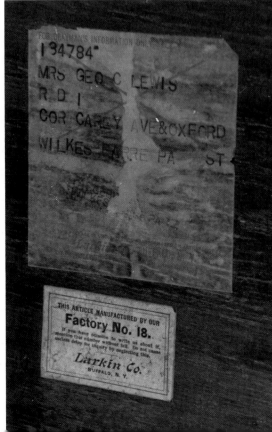

CHINA, CURIOS

Bowed sides and a slightly bowed door enclose this china cabinet supported by claw-footed legs. $1,400

However small, (29" wide x 62" tall x 9" deep) this bowed glass curio cabinet displays a bentwood structure and intricate spindles. It remains in its original finish. $1,400

The mirrored back and glass shelves (not shown) of this 36" wide curio cabinet are enclosed by a bowed glass door flanked by carved, open mouthed lion heads. $1,500

Four large carved claw feet support this china closet with bowed glass enclosing oak shelves. Quartered oak grain is vibrant on the door frame and columns. A molded top and large beveled mirror complete the design. $1,800

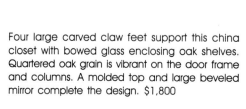

Glass shelves and mirrored back displays treasured items beautifully within the bowed glass sides and straight glass door of this china closet. A jester is carved on the crest. Lion heads flow into claw feet standing on rope-twisted columns, decorating each side of the door. $5,000

Bowed sides and a serpentined door with green-tinted glass encloses the mirrored back and crystal shelves of this china closet. Carved lion heads stand on round claw feet. $4,000

A carved half-figure angel spreads wings amidst scroll carvings within the dome above a bowed door in this china closet. Quarter-sawn veneer columns flank bowed sides above claw feet. $4,800

The molded top of this china closet displays a grotesque masque at the crest. Tapered rope-twists trim the door and deeply bowed sides which rest above a drawer and claw feet. $3,900

Corinthian capital decorate the columns flanking the bowed door and bowed sides of this 36" china cabinet. Standing 65" tall x 15" deep, it rests on diagonally set claw feet that curve from beneath the columns. The four oak shelves are not in place. $1,900

Serpentined glass shimmers between the quarter-cut veneered columns and bowed glass sides of this china closet. An elaborately carved, triple-mirrored gallery rests upon the curved top which supports a carved winged lion's head. $5,000

Double beveled glass doors and sides enclose this elegant curio cabinet. Corner columns rest upon carved caryatids and flow gracefully to the floor into clawfeet. $4,500

Grotesque carved figures on elaborately shaped columns seem to guard the serpentine glass door of this bowed china closet as it stands on massive clawfeet. $4,800

Glass sides, side lights and a center glass door enclose this rectangular china closet with mirrored top shelf. Decorated corner posts and molding add interest to this design. $1,500

Music Room

The phonograph produces sounds by means of the vibration of a stylus, or needle following a groove on a rotating disk or cylinder.

Experimental mechanisms of this type appeared as early as 1857. The invention of the phonograph is credited to the United States inventor, Thomas Edison, in 1877.

All modern phonographs have certain components in common: a turntable that spins the record; a stylus that converts the mechanical movements of the stylus into electrical impulses; and a loudspeaker that converts the amplified signals back into sound.

A phonograph capable of undistorted reproduction of sound is one component of what is known as a high-fidelity sound system and is an integral part of our lives today.

The Victor Victrola VI was offered as home entertainment during the years 1911 through 1926. The horn has now disappeared as the sound emerges from the face of the oak cabinet (15¼" wide x 16 ³/₈" deep x 8½" high) through the exhibition soundbox.

A double spring motor drives the 12" diameter turntable as the hollow nickel plated tone arm holds the needle as it glides along the grooves of the disc producing the sound. The model shown sold for $25.00 to $35.00, around 1915. Collection of Robert Stull. $450

Thomas Edison's Model D"Home Graphophone," known as the "talking machine," brought expressions of talented strangers into the American homes. Words and songs imprinted on wax cylinders could be enjoyed repeatedly. Two to four cylinders could be played with one winding.

The handsome Cygnet horn, the name derived from the French word "Cygne" meaning "Swan," stands to a height of 39" to broadcast the sounds as the cylinders revolve. The ten panel metal horn is painted black with gold striping. It could be removed when not in use. The 16½" wide by 9½" deep by 5¾" high oak base, supporting the talking machine, was covered with its bent oak cover equipped with a handle forming a convenient carrying case. Available 1909 through 1911.

The phonograph, Thomas Edison's most original invention, was achieved when some unexpected phenomenon was observed as he worked on another project. It was based on a fresh observation of the dynamics of sound in 1877. Edison had enjoyed a high repute among American technicians up to this time, but the invention of the phonograph made him internationally famous. The embryonic phonograph was Edison's favorite of his 1,093 patents, among which was also the invention of the incandescent electric lamp. These two inventions alone changed the ways of living tremendously. Collection of Robert Stull. $1,300

GRAMOPHONE

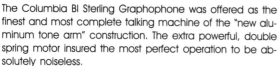

The Columbia BI Sterling Graphophone was offered as the finest and most complete talking machine of the "new aluminum tone arm" construction. The extra powerful, double spring motor insured the most perfect operation to be absolutely noiseless.

The 13" square by 7⅝" high quarter-sawn oak cabinet with its ornamental design reads "The Columbia Disc Graphophonic Columbia Phonograph Co." The front label states "The Graphophone and Columbia records were awarded The Grand Prize at The Paris Exhibition of 1900, The St. Louis Exposition of 1904 and the Milan Exposition of 1906." The beautiful floral designed horn resembles a great morning glory with its nine-panel, highly polished, nickelplated, brass finish which contributed greatly to the perfection of sound reproduction and to the ornamental appearance of the machine.

The aluminum tone arm was the greatest improvement as this construction gave the greatest possible volume of sound, the clearest and most natural reproduction with the finest and most perfect music quality.

Offered by Sear Roebuck Catalog, it is shown in 1909 for $45.00 Collection of Robert Stull. $1,500

Columbia Phonograph Company of New York offered this floor model during the years of 1915 through 1917. The free-standing quarter-sawn oak cabinet (42¾" tall x 18½" wide x 20½" deep) housed the 11½" diameter turnable beneath its lift-up lid. The sound radiated from the face of the cabinet when the lower doors were opened for the desired volume. Storage for additional records was provided behind double doors beneath the voicebox. An original label remains on the bottom stating "It shall be sold for $75.00". Collection of Robert Stull. $700

The Pease Piano Company of New York offered this beautiful "Cabinet Grand" upright piano in 1902. The date was established by researching the serial number.
Carved panels decorate the face of the burled oak veneer case. The unusual grain pattern is outstanding in artistic design. The ivory and ebony keyboard is supported by fluted columns duplicated on the legs of the piano bench. Round corners curve to meet the raised panel sides.
Chauncy B. Pease established the company in 1844. It was sold in 1949. Collection of Robert and Lisa Stull. $4,000

Beautifully preserved, this elaborately decorated Beckwith Parlor Reed organ remains in its immaculate original finish. It is in unrestored working condition. Advertised in the 1908 Sears catalog as being superior to any other organ. Two full pages were devoted to the merits of Beckwith Reed organs.

Anyone can play if one is able to co-ordinate the eyes to read the music, the fingers to play the notes, the feet to pump the bellows, and the knees to operate the swell rods...and, of course, sing along at the same time. Good luck!

This center attraction parlor organ offered entertainment along with its outstanding decorative qualities in its 88" high by 44" wide cabinet, constructed in two pieces. $4,000 mint condition.

219

BECKWITH ORGANS
HIGHEST AWARD ST. LOUIS WORLD'S FAIR ~ AND JAMESTOWN EXPOSITION

A MAGNIFICENT LINE OF REED ORGANS

Manufactured in the most modern, up to date and best equipped organ factories in the world, and which for durability of construction, refinement and elegance of appearance, beauty of finish and musical capacity, are superior to any other organs made.

THE BECKWITH ORGAN COMPANY have established two of the very largest organ factories in the world for the sole purpose of manufacturing these splendid instruments. These factories are complete in every detail. In them they have installed the very latest, most improved labor saving organ making machinery and the very best system of handling material. They have enormous quantities of selected lumber on hand going through the long process of air seasoning. They have immense dry kilns, thus insuring wood for use in the organs that is absolutely and perfectly bone dry. They employ the most skillful, most experienced workman and use the most rigid system of inspection. These organ factories are located at two points, one at Louisville, Kentucky, the other at St. Paul, Minnesota, and in this way we are in a position to make a very large saving on the freight charges on any organ ordered from us. Our enormous organ business is not the result of chance or a favorable combination of circumstances, but has been built up through a most careful and conscientious attention to the smallest detail, unremitting and untiring efforts to maintain the exalted quality of these organs, which years ago secured recognition from prominent authorities as the finest organs in the world. The result is the most enviable reputation enjoyed by any like instruments in the market.

THE BECKWITH ORGANS are manufactured under our direct supervision, are fully guaranteed by us for twenty-five years and are sold only from factory to customer direct and in no other way, at the actual factory cost with our uniformly one small margin of profit added; under the most liberal terms and free trial offers ever made, as fully explained in detail on page 209 of this catalogue. You are fully protected when you place an order for a Beckwith Organ from the following pages. You secure every benefit that we, ourselves, can secure in the way of price reducing methods of manufacture. Every bit of saving that can be effected in any way goes to you because we are content to receive our usual one small margin of profit and, therefore, this organ, which is the standard of organ quality for the world, is placed in your home at actually less cost to you than others ask for inferior instruments of much less musical capacity.

THE MATERIALS are all the best that can be purchased by experts in their line. Each piece of wood is selected for its fitness, perfection of grain and fiber before it is accepted as fit for use in the Beckwith. All felts, reeds, springs, even the glue, varnish, etc., are all carefully inspected before accepted and the methods of construction and the check upon the quality of material purchased, put into effect by the Beckwith Organ Company, enable us to unqualifiedly guarantee these organs against any defect in their material or workmanship for a full quarter of a century.

THE QUESTION OF QUALITY is one that you should fully consider before you place your order. An agent unknown to you may place an organ in your home today that looks and sounds well, and to all appearances you have every reason to believe that it will prove "a thing of beauty and a joy forever," but tomorrow, next week, next month, perhaps, after the agent has gone, then the real trial of the organ will begin. Will it prove entirely satisfactory? Is there a lasting quality to its tone? If any defect should manifest itself, if you have any complaint to make of any nature, to whom will you go for redress? What guarantee do you hold? Where is the agent or manufacturer who gave the guarantee? What satisfaction will you secure in case you have any grievance to make? These things should all be considered when you place your order. If you do not favor us, then you should be sure of the guarantee. Buy an organ that is guaranteed by a responsible company who has money invested in a business, who will be here today, next year, twenty-five years from today, a concern backed by a large capital, responsibility and a reputation for fair dealing and you will run no risk. But in justice to yourself you ought first to try a Beckwith under our liberal terms before considering any other organ of any other make. Simply because our prices represent more of a saving to you than any other prices quoted by anyone on a **high grade** organ, and because we positively take the risk.

Facsimile of the great Diploma of Merit awarded the Beckwith Organs at the St. Louis World's Fair.

THE GOLD MEDAL UNANIMOUSLY VOTED TO THE BECKWITH ORGANS

ALL DOUBT AS TO THE QUALITY of the Beckwith has been forever removed, because of the special honors heaped upon it at the two greatest exhibitions of the product of man's ingenuity of recent years. It received the highest medal and diploma of merit and other honors at the St. Louis World's Fair and at the great Jamestown Exposition just closed, the **Gold Medal** was unanimously conferred upon this organ by the judges, together with other very special honors that fully attests its superlative quality. The magnificent line of Beckwith Parlor, Church and Chapel Organs shown at these two great exhibits attracted world wide attention and in each instance the highest honors were unanimously voted them in competition with a number of other organs of world renowned make, thus removing for all time all doubt, if any doubt had existed, as to the wonderfully high quality and the exalted excellence represented in the

IF YOU WISH TO SAVE MONEY, if you desire to take advantage of our great money saving prices and liberal offers, testing the organ in your own home for full thirty days at our risk, then do not let any agent or anyone else interested in seeing you buy some other organ at a profit or commission to themselves, argue you out of it. Do not be deceived by those who advance arguments against your own interests, who advise you not to save money on the purchase of an organ, but who advise you to buy elsewhere at a larger price. There is no mystery or secret processes in making an organ and we challenge the world to produce an organ equal to the Beckwith in quality and tone. Remember that those who would advise you not to try a Beckwith at our risk, with the understanding that you are not asked to buy it unless it represents a wonderful saving, are not advising you for your own interests. All we ask of you is that we be permitted to answer any argument made against the Beckwith. If you

LOUISVILLE FACTORY.

ST. PAUL FACTORY.

Beckwith. This organ stands upon the highest pinnacle of musical excellence, and to question the quality in this organ means to cast reflection upon the integrity, honesty of purpose and sound judgment of the two great international juries, made up of the most distinguished and eminent authorities on organ construction and quality, who were unanimous in conferring these honors upon the Beckwith Organ, not only at the St. Louis World's Fair, but the Jamestown Exposition as well. Wherever the Beckwith Organ has been entered in competition with other well known makes, it invariably carries off the highest honors and it is recognized and acknowledged to be the standard of organ quality for the entire world. Others may copy the Beckwith Organ cases and the magnificent finish and appearance they represent, but no manufacturer has yet been able to imitate the wonderful tone quality.

WHY ARE YOU READING THIS PAGE?
We feel sure that it is because you are interested either today, tomorrow or at some future time in the purchase of an organ. We would be very much pleased to prove to you the truth of our claims regarding the Beckwith Organ, to prove to you the excellence of these instruments by sending any one you may select for a complete thirty-day trial under our "send no money offer." If you will consent to our placing one of these organs in your home on trial, we are so sure that you will agree to keep it at the end of the trial term and give it your heartiest endorsement as well, that we will be perfectly willing to accept your order under our liberal terms and send it to you, freight charges prepaid, taking all the risk and responsibility without a single penny being advanced by you, as fully described on page 209. It has been proved that wherever we sell a Beckwith Organ we make a great many good friends, and the consequence is increased orders for this instrument. Therefore, it is very profitable to us to accept a very little margin of profit on each instrument, owing to the thousands and thousands we sell every year.

will order an instrument on trial at our risk, you would soon be convinced that if anyone advises you not to buy a Beckwith, but to buy some other make of organ at double our prices, that they are not advising you for your own welfare. They are not advising you to buy where you can get the greatest degree of satisfaction and value at the smallest possible price, therefore at the greater saving to you.

LET US PROVE THAT IT IS THE FINEST INSTRUMENT EVER OFFERED.
This you can easily do without any risk to yourself. Try a Beckwith Organ at our risk, and if you do not find it all we claim it to be, then send it back and buy from someone else at a much larger price, therefore, at a larger cost to you. You owe it to yourself to take advantage of our prices and liberal offers. If any argument is advanced as to why you should not save for yourself all that our prices mean, then please let us answer every statement made to you against our money saving prices and liberal terms. If you are looking for an organ at all, it is only natural that you should be looking for the best it is possible to secure. Remember the special honors conferred on the Beckwith at the St. Louis World's Fair and the Jamestown Exposition. Again, it is natural that if you want to save as much money as is possible in the transaction. That being the case you cannot afford to overlook our offers. Nowhere can you get such a fine organ and so much value and musical capacity at such a saving in price. In view of these facts, in view of the liberal shipping terms, under which we gladly send out the Beckwith Organs, in view of our strong guarantee backed by Forty Million Dollars' worth of capital, do you not owe it to yourself, you who are reading this page, to order a Beckwith Organ on trial, so as to prove to your complete satisfaction whether or not our claims are true, whether or not we can save you one-half on the purchase of a high grade instrument?

SMALL CHESTS

Eight shallow drawers are concealed within the door of this small, undecorated cabinet. A single, larger drawer is in view to give 33" of storage space. The 16 x 20 quartered oak top is nicely beveled along the edges. $650

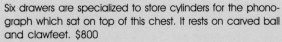

Six drawers are specialized to store cylinders for the phonograph which sat on top of this chest. It rests on carved ball and clawfeet. $800

Solid, quartered oak was used to build this small chest. The two drawers are actually pull-out files for documents or magazines. It stands on straight legs. $500

LIBRARY DESKS

The surface of this library desk is solid, quarter-sawn oak. Cabriole legs and concave stretchers support a shelf. The apron conceals a center drawer. $750

Square reeded legs join the corners of this library desk with boss mounts flanking the center drawer. $800

This library desk has solid quartered oak on its surface and rolled apron. It has carved and cabriole legs with claw feet. $800

The curved legs and shaped shelf add grace to this small library desk with a center drawer. $400

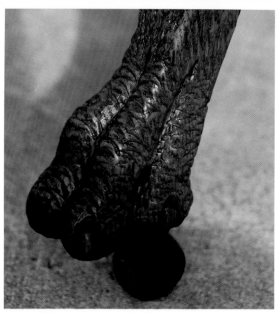

Solid quartered oak in this library desk has a beveled edge above the scalloped apron and full-width drawer. Cabriole legs with scaled, claw feet are joined by a rectangular shelf and stretchers. Fancy brass pulls decorate the drawer. $900

The turtle-shaped top of this library desk is distinctive. The apron adds depth and encloses a drawer. Legs curve to meet the shelf below. $900

The carved top and apron of this library desk accentuate large, rope-twisted legs strengthened by rope-twisted stretchers. $1,900

Solid quartered oak radiates on the pressed top of this long and narrow library desk. The pressed apron conceals a center drawer. Double fluted turnings decorate round legs which support a wide, scalloped shelf. $1,400

A center drawer is framed by two decorated square drawers beneath the solid, quarter-sawn top of this library desk. Rope-twisted legs support caned end panels and a caned shelf. $1,900

The English Chippendale style is reflected in this narrow library desk. Gadrooned edges accent the top with a center shell carving and bright, brass pulls. Cabriole legs with ball and claw feet support the front while straight legs support the back. It is possible that originally this was a partners' desk which has been cut in half. $1,000

Vividly striped in its solid quarter-sawn oak, this library desk stands on its capriole legs as they curve outward from the corners, inward to meet the shaped shelf and outward to meet the floor in unusual squared feet. $800

BOOKCASES

This cute, two-level, sectional bookcase rests on a sculptured base with an S-curved top. It bears a gold decal marked: "Macey." $600

This cute, bookcase, with incised scroll carving, folds flat. The shelves are pinned to revolve upward when the front legs are lifted. $400

This single, glass-enclosed bookcase has a simple carved trim above the door. $700

Triple glass doors enclosed this five-feet-wide bookcase. Adjustable shelves fit independently within each section. $1,800

This bookcase also folds. The shelves are pinned to revolve up and the sides are hinged to fold toward the center. $950

This small 36"-wide bookcase is enclosed by double leaded glass doors. $900

Stained, leaded glass enhances the double doors of this 42"-wide bookcase resting on scrolled feet. It is shown in the 1909 Larkin Soap Co. catalog as "Bookcase No. 710" which was exchanged for ten Larkin certificates. $1,800

Shell carvings and columns flank the double glass doors to enhance this bookcase. $1,500

Lion's heads decorate the shaped door frames of this bookcase. Scroll carvings on the rounded corners add to its beauty and double drawers provide additional storage. $1,800

Elegantly styled, this high-grade bookcase, in an immaculate, original finish, has edge trim on its double glass doors. The rounded corners are decorated and the shaped top adds to its beauty. $1,800

Carved claw feet support this triple bookcase which is otherwise decorated only by its quartered oak grain and rolled edges. $2,000

Acid-etched glass panels add interest to the outside doors of this triple bookcase. A closed center compartment with decoratively carved door and drawer provide hidden storage. $2,200

A bookcase of five units with a sculptured base and cap, 76" high. It is stamped: "Gunn Sectional Bookcase, Gunn Furniture Co., Grand Rapids, Michigan." $1,600

Four units of different sizes comprise this "Globe Wernicke" sectional bookcase, 57" high. The square-legged base contains a drawer and a square cap rest on the top. $1,300

Five leaded glass units stand on a sculptured base in this sectional bookcase marked: "Globe Wernicke." $2,800

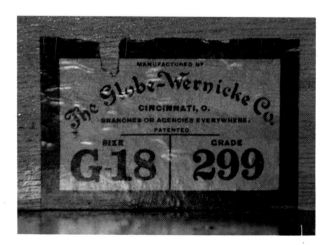

Two 18"-wide units comprise this Globe Wernicke Co. sectional bookcase with a sculptured cap and base with a drawer. $1,200

This three-level "Macy" sectional bookcase rests on a base with ball and claw feet and a drawer. $1,100

Enhanced by the shaped side boards and molded trim beneath the top shelf, this 30"-wide x 56" tall, open bookcase provides five levels for book storage with its three adjustable center shelves. The scalloped floor board adds to its character. $900

Triple glass door enclose a collection of crystal and blue delft cherished by the owners. Also cherished is the bookcase itself, now a curio as it displays its carvings across the top above the doors and down the beveled corners. "Northwind" frowns above the center door as his moustache flows outward into scrolls. Bun feet support the 74" wide x 50" tall x 14" deep case and its contents. $2,800

Five units, including a drop-front desk, compromise this Globe Wernicke Co. sectional bookcase. The two lower bookcase units place the desk at a convenient writing height while the two upper units remain accessible. $1,800

The original finish maintains its gloss on the units of this "Globe-Wernicke" sectional bookcase. The legged base supports the 9", 11", and much desired 13" units beneath the squared top. Well kept during its lifetime, the quartered oak stripes continue to shine through the clear finish. Notice the absence of side straps as are found on similar bookcases having sculpture bases and tops. $950

Four units comprise this sectional bookcase with a dropfront desk. The leaded unit accents the combination and sculptured top and base. $1,800

Original finish remains on the "Globe-Wernicke" sectional bookcase. 34" wide being standard width, the three 10¼" cases with the sculptured base housing a drawer and the sculptured top stand 47" in height. Similar bookcases easily vary in height depending on the height of each individual section. When originally sold, units could be purchased so that their sizes were uniform. Many bookcases could be interlocked side by side to construct an entire wall of bookcases if desired. The side strapping provided the interlocking device. $1,000 refinished.

MORRIS CHAIRS

Morris chair has a recently upholstered spring seat and back surrounded by broad shaped arms supported by seven rope-twisted spindles and a larger armpost. Openwork trims the shaped face board. Shaped legs have softened (contoured) clawfeet. $850

Outstanding matched pair "Globe-Wernicke" sectional bookcases. Seven 10¼" units comprise each case resting upon the sculptured base housing a drawer with the sculptured top reaching eight feet. Immaculate original finish remains. $4,500 pair.

Platform Morris recliner rocker has broad contoured arms with curved arm supports flowing over the quartered face board. The chair rocks upon a clawfooted platform. $800

This heavy, solid-quartered oak Morris recliner has broad, shaped arms culminating in outrageous faces. The arm supports glide into huge, carved clawfeet. $1,200

Giant, curved arms roll forward to open-mouthed lion heads above the elaborately scrolled case board, supported by fluted ball feet. $1,500

Kitchen

SQUARE LEGGED TABLES

Tapered, turned, and fluted legs with carved stretchers accent this 44" wide, solid quartered table with three 12" wide extension leaves. $1,200

Quarter grain is radiant on the 48"-square table top and its shaped apron. Large, claw-footed, fluted legs are joined by a concave stretcher. $1,500

Beehive-shaped legs and large claw feet support this 44"-square dining table with grooved apron. $1,500

Five, large, turned and fluted legs support the 45"-square straight-grained top of this table with a molded apron. $1,600

Five, shaped, turned and fluted legs support the 48"-square top of this solid quartered table. The five extension leaves continue the rounded edges, shaped band with tiny rope-twisted trim, and carved corners of the top. $2,000

Above and left:
Turned, contoured, and fluted legs elegantly support this 42"-square dining table with five extension leaves. It was made by National Furniture Co. of Williamsport, PA.

Round, claw feet rest on tapered, fluted legs to support the 46"-square top of this table which has three 10" wide leaves. $1,200

Tapered, rope-twisted , turned legs and knobby, claw feet accentuate this 44"-square table with a tapered, molded apron. Three 10" long leaves expand the top. $1,800

Rope-twisted, claw-footed legs decorate this 44"-square dining table. Its rounded, ribbed apron extends with the addition of two 13" wide leaves. $1,900

This 48"-square, solid quartered oak dining table has formal design. Its cabriole legs curve gracefully and end in ball and claw feet. $1,900

The giant, turned and fluted legs make this 42"-square table appear small. However, when the leaves extend the top, the legs are in better proportion. $1,800 with 4 leaves.

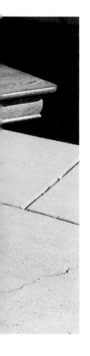

Three sets of double turned legs are joined by spindle stretchers on this square dining table. Flower carved corners and a grooved apron enhance its beauty. $1,600

Intricately carved, shaped, and fluted legs with claw feet support this 45"-square dining table with feather-carved apron and four extension leaves. $1,600

Four, large, S-curved, claw-footed legs protrude from the support of this 45"-square dining table. A conservatively turned middle leg supports the center when three 10" wide leaves are added. $1,800

The unusual bamboo design of this table's center stretcher panel set between square, reeded legs is interesting. The top has rounded corners and a grooved apron with corner medallions. $1,200

The six, turned, straight legs are joined by grooved, concave stretchers and decorated with brass-trimmed, turned spindlework which dress up this otherwise plain table. $1,400

Five fat, turned, tapered, and fluted legs are particularly graceful beneath this 46"-square, solid quartered oak dining table. The top has two, 10"-wide leaves. The straight apron also has quartered grain. $1,600

Open oak grain decorates the molded band of this 42"-sqaure dining table on turned and fluted legs with claw feet. Five 10"-wide leaves rest on the extension slides. It is signed "Watsontown Table Co." $2,100 with five leaves, signed.

Five, large, turned and fluted legs support this 42"-square, solid quartered oak table top. It is enhanced by the shaped apron with incised carving at the corners. Five, 9½"-wide leaves expand the table. $1,600

Open oak grain is displayed on the 42"-square top of this dining table which is supported by five turned and rope-twisted legs. The slides extend to accommodate the extension leaves. $1,500

Five turned, tapered and fluted legs support the 42"-square, solid quartered top of this dining table with a molded band. Five matching leaves expand its usefulness. $1,400

Vibrant quartered grain was used to make the top of this dining table. Its beaded apron and carved corners set off the turned and fluted legs and claw feet legs. Five leaves can be added over the slides to extend the top. $1,800

Four fluted and turned legs with claw feet are joined by concave, double-beaded stretchers. Two plain, fluted legs support the center. $1,200

A scroll-pressed apron and capped, fluted corners decorate this dining table. Pairs of turned and square fluted legs joined by decorated concave stretchers support the top and four extension leaves. $1,400

Five enormous, turned, carve, shaped and fluted legs rest beneath the 49"-wide top of this dining table. Carved and rounded corners accentuate the rounded edge of the top. $2,100

Incredible detail as the center supporting turned legs set between two separate square pillars of this Eastlake style table. Incised carving accents the squared legs which protrude form the pillars diagonally toward the corners to support the top with large beehive turnings. The shaped and grooved band has corner trimmings and moldings at the center divide. Upon opening, the double pillars separate to accommodate the four 12½" leaves. $2,800

Six spiral, bulbous legs with large and deep turnings are joined by spooled, concave and scroll-decorated stretchers to support this 48"-wide, solid, quartered oak top and six 12"-wide quartered oak leaves. The deeply molded apron is further embellished by a large, rope-twisted lower edge. $2,900

Solid, quarter-sawn oak was chosen for the top of this 45"-wide, square dining table with rounded, carved corners and a sculptured apron. Carved, S-curved legs, and claw feet are joined by concave stretchers. Double plain legs support the center when the four, 12"-wide quarter-sawn leaves are added. $2,500

Incised lines and circles decorate the apron of this 48"-square, solid quartered oak dining table. The six turned and fluted legs are joined by stretchers. Four extension leaves can be added. $1,200

ROUND LEGGED TABLES

Five turned and rope-twisted legs support the 44" diameter top to this dining table which has three extension leaves. $1,200

Claw feet with thin, tapered, fluted ankles gracefully supporting the round top of this dining table. A fine rope-twist trims the apron. $1,500

Turned and reeded legs enhance the country charm of this 42" diameter, round table with three extension leaves. $1,000 table, $900 set of four chairs, see page 64 top left.

Five large, turned, tapered and fluted legs support the 45" diameter top of this dining table with three extension leaves. The co-ordinated chairs show quartered oak grain on the headpiece and shaped lower rail. This plain, but elegant, chair has a full boxed seat which adds to its strength, as additional support, joining the tapered legs along with the H-rungs. $1,500 table, $1,500 set of 6 chairs.

Heavy, bowed and claw-footed legs protrude from the support of this 45" diameter, round, solid quartered table which has a wide decorated apron. Four quartered leaves extend this table to an elongated oval. Matching upholstered chairs have been retained with the table. $2,500

Simple in style and plain in appearance, this 36" round table stands firm on square legs. Ideal for a small space, possibly dressed up with pressedback chairs. $350 table, see page 66 center far right.

HOOSIER CUPBOARDS

The center camboured roll-up door of this "Sellers" kitchen cupboard is surround by beautifully grained cabinet doors which enclose a flour sifter on the left and a sugar bin on the right. Two utensil drawers are mounted beneath the 48" wide porcelain pullout work surface. An additional storage cabinet and drawers are in the base. $2,500

Blue grass-enclosed doors surround the vertical roll in this kitchen cabinet. Three drawers and an enclosed storage area are in the base cabinet. $1,200

Etched and frosted glass enclosed doors hang over double doors closing to the center on this kitchen cabinet. The pullout work surface is of oak, below are additional storage compartments. $1,200

Slag glass decorates the cabinet doors of the "Marsh Konvenient Kitchen Kabinet, form High Point, N. Carolina." Its original decal is intact, along with a "Good House-keeping Magazine Seal of Approval" label within a drawer. $2,000

The center cabinet door with decorated glass and lattice work is framed by the domed top and curved cabinet doors. The tan pullout porcelain work area has a brown edge. The door handles are the original red Bakelite. The base offers a tall cupboard and four drawers. $1,600

CUPBOARDS

Unusually large, this laboratory cupboard has many shelves displayed behind two pairs of sliding glass doors. The base contains six large drawers and two storage areas enclosed by double doors. Signed "Kewaunee Manufacturing Co. Laboratory Furniture Experts Kewaunee, Wisconsin." $4,500

Opposite page top right:
This giant enclosed laboratory cupboard is shown with its old varnish removed. The two sets of double doors enclose storage shelves. The base cabinet conceals two pull-out tablets under the lip above the lower doors. It awaits stain and a new finish. $2,600

Opposite page bottom right:
Once a display case in a Lancaster, PA department store, this ten feet wide by eight feet tall breakfront now displays china and crystal behind glass doors. The base has a center storage cabinet with drawers on each side and decorated with burled veneer panels. $6,500

This page right:
Inset domed panels and ovals add style to this tall cupboard. The double doors are separated by small shelves and two tiny drawers. The raised top provides a platform on the base cabinet which contains two cutlery drawers and a large enclosed storage compartment. $2,600

This step-back cupboard has shaped double glass doors with two small drawers resting upon the base with a full width drawer and enclosed storage area. A small molding and applied scroll carving decorate the top. $1,800

This straight-front cupboard has visible storage through double glass doors. Two drawers for utensils rest above an enclosed storage area. Paneled side add strength and the incised crest adds a touch of decoration. $1,200

The 52" face of this seven feet tall corner cupboard displays ribbon carving above its single glass door. The curio shelf is backed, on the diagonals, with beveled mirrors. Ribbon carving again enhances the face above the double raised panel doors as shaped half-columns decorate each side. $4,500

Double beveled glass doors, a molded top, a beveled mirrored back and crystal shelves make up the 8½ feet tall corner cabinet. Below, deeply cut raised panels enhance the double doors. $4,500

This large, undecorated step-back cupboard originally served as a commercial storage unit. The tall, glass-enclosed top is twice the height on the enclosed base. The owner's prized items are displayed behind the glass doors, but the cupboard is their "prize." Purchased in 1979, they have carefully moved it many times from state to state, along with the family. $3,500

ICEBOXES

This icebox by the Gurney Refrigerator Co. of Ronddulac, Wisconsin retains its original name plate, patent number, and date. An oval plate also states that it was "Manufactured expressly for N. Snellenburg & Co. Philadelphia, PA." Quartered oak recessed panels enhance three doors set in their open grained frames with brass spring latches. 41" tall with castors x 31" wide x 17" deep. $1,800

Scroll carvings applied to the refrigerator door panels and to the center panel above add touches of elegance to this top-loading icebox. The lift-up top divides the molded trim. The drip pan flap, brass hinges and latch continue the dressed-up styling. $1,200

Open oak grain was used on this vertical, top-loading icebox, giving life to its simple design. Shaped brass hinges and latch accent the door of the galvanized tin lined refrigerator compartment. A small, plain handle lifts the top to receive the block of ice. $1,000

Recess paneled doors enclose the white porcelain interior of this icebox by the Baldwin Refrigerator Co. of Burlington, VT. Brass roller latches, shaped hinges, a molded top and wide open oak grain set off the front. The sides are flat panels, not of oak. $1,800

Quartered oak grain radiates on the door panels of this white porcelain-lined icebox. The interior is in immaculate, original condition. $1,600

The doors of this porcelain-lined icebox are reinforced with center stiles in addition to the normal door structure, giving the face a distinctive look set off by shaped, brass hinges and latches. $1,800

Raised panels decorate the two doors of this icebox with recessed panels decorating the sides, as they provide strong construction. The ice block placed in the upper compartment provided the cold to refrigerate the food contained below. As the ice melted, the water flowed through a tube for collection in a pan located under the icebox and concealed by the lift-up floorboard. $1,400

The return from several days away from home often times presented a flooded kitchen. One family remedied the problem by drilling a hole in the kitchen floor, draining the water into a barrel located in the basement.

Fancy, spring loaded brass latches secure the triple doors of this 34" wide x 45" tall x 18½" deep icebox. The ice compartment at the upper left is lined with galvanized tin. Being heavy, cold air maintained the compartment below as the coldest area. The cold flowed to the refrigerator portion through the oval holes provided in the interior dividing wall. If the arms were full, the spring latches allowed the doors to be closed with a "flip of the hip." $1,800

Bedroom

BEDS

Ornately carved, seven foot tall bed with elaborate scrolls duplicated on the curved head and footboards. $1,800

Heavy leaf carvings crown the head of this otherwise plain bed. $1,400

The four foot headboard exhibits the result of "cutting down" a bed to use it in a room with a low ceiling. The sideposts were cut to shorten the height, preserving the scroll-carved top panel. The footboard was evidently discarded. $500

Delicate scroll carvings accentuate the curving lines cresting this headboard, with footboard and sideposts also scroll carved. $1,200

A handsome rolled and scrolled bed has decorated headboard with a half roll at the center. Wide panels show their quarter grain. The rolled footboard is carved to compliment the head board. $1,600

Delicately scrolled quarter-sawn bed. The panels are broad and vibrantly grained. Applied carving at the center headboard conceals the joining of the upper and lower panels. Notice the grain pattern as it takes the eye up and around to the crest. $1,800

Open straight grain dominates wide panels as a center half roll and heavy scroll carvings decorate the crest of this tall bed. The rolled footboard displays a complimentary carving as it appears to support the roll. $1,800

Unadorned bed of quarter-sawn, grain-matched veneer in a simple style. $1,400

The vibrant quarter grain radiates on the matched, delicately carved and rolled head and footboards of this bed. $1,200

A fluted half-roll with long curled ends flows into scrolled carving as it decorates the crest. The footboard has a wide top rail, but is undecorated. $1,600

Barely decorated headboard shows multiple open-grained panels. Footboard was unavailable. $800

Broad, quartered panels are accentuated by delicate scroll carvings on the head and footboard of this lower bed. $1,200

Tall, rolled headboard and footboard displays wide quartered and straight grain panels. $1,900

Elegant quartered bed is decorated by a center carving with flowing scrolls accentuating the crest. $1,600

Gracefully curved and carved bed displays broad quartered panels, with a shaped raised panel at the center headboard. $1,500

Quartered oval panels dominate the 54" headboard and matching footboard of this elegant bed. Scroll carvings accentuate the lower corners of the ovals. $1,600

Beautifully scroll-carved raised panel bed with shaped crest and sideposts duplicates the pattern on its raised-panel footboard. $1,900

Shaped center crest flows softly to the sidepost carvings framing the top panel's scrolled decoration. A shallow raised panel adds interest to the second panel and to the footboard. $1,800

Exceptionally heavy, this 60" tall bed displays beaded trim across the straight outline of this molded head and footboards. Heavy carving accentuates the center, deeply cut, raised panel of the headboard with a duplicate raised panel on the footboard. $1,400

BEDS/TWIN

This Eastlake style, single bed, characterized by its incised carvings and grooved lines, displays its tall crescent crest protruding over the incised carved daisy and leaf pattern of the headboard. The footboard duplicated the design. $1,600

Handsomely decorated, the vertical panels on the head and footboards create a unique look on this youth bed, which is six inches wider and six inches shorter than a regular single. $1,400

The shaped crest is the simple decoration on this 55" tall single bed headboard. Accomodating today's single mattress, this same style has come along as Youth-size bed being shorter and wider and requiring custom bedding, but providing a wider bed for a child. $900

Applied scroll carving with a center flower decorates the shaped crest of this single oak bed. The second panel is double grooved. The grooving on the footboard adds interest. $1,200

The scrolled crest is connected to each side by a touch of incised carving on this single oak bed. $1,200

BLANKET CHESTS

Set-in panels and quartered oak grain decorate this blanket chest. Chests of this size are often used as coffee tables. $800

Copper strapping set with brass rivets wraps around this oak blanket chest. $900

DRESSERS

This exceptionally wide dresser displays a large, beveled mirror above slightly protruding, curved drawers. The uprights curve outwardly, tapering into carved clawfeet. A quartered veneer pattern decorates the face. $1,300

The large, oval, beveled mirror stands 71" tall in a shaped harp above the 44" wide triple serpentined chest, supported by carved clawfeet. $1,200

The tall, crested, oval mirror stands above the straight front chest of drawers which is decorated only by its hardware. $900

Elaborate applied scroll carvings decorate the mirror and harp of this open grained oak dresser. Gently shaped drawer fronts and fancy brass pulls compliment the mirror. $1,500

Solid quartered oak with distinct grain was chosen for this 83½" tall dresser. Carved ribbons and garlands drape the large dome-top, beveled mirror. The 48" wide chest protrudes at the corners above columns extending to the floor, forming the legs. $1,500

The drop of this 48" wide dresser accentuates the cantilever beveled mirrors as it is framed between two glove drawers above the wide concave curve of the chest. The cantilever mirrors swing to allow better viewing. Shaped legs and carved clawfeet support this elegant dresser. Signed Estey Manufacturing Co., Owasso, Michigan. $2,500

Incised flowers and leaves decorate the harp and drawers of this Estlake style dresser. $900

The shaped, beveled mirror of this dresser with its scroll-carved and harp rests upon the triple serpentined two-over-four-drawer chest. $1,100

Interesting carvings decorate the mirror and harp of this triple serpentined dresser with carved clawfeet. $1,600

Double boxes rest upon the wide low chest of this princess dresser. The rectangular, beveled mirror is suspended in the carved enclosed harp. $1,400

Scroll carvings and the shaped beveled mirror of this dresser enhance the slightly bowed chest of drawers. $1,200

The large, oval, beveled mirror with carved crest and scroll-carved harp rests above the low, wide serpentined chest of this Princess dresser supported by carved clawfeet. $1,500

The convex front of this vibrantly grained quartered oak veneered princess dress swells between carved clawfeet. The tall shaped beveled mirror is suspended by its harp resting upon two jewelry drawers. Collection of Lisa and Robert Stull. $1,300

Applied scroll carvings decorate the mirror harp's crest on this Cheval dresser. A glove drawer and hat box offset the mirror as it sits upon a low, shaped chest. The high bed seen in the background co-ordinated to make a set. $1,500

The tall, oval, beveled mirror is suspended in a curved harp above the low chest of this princess dresser. $800

The double arched crest crowns the beveled mirror of this dresser with its S-curved drawers, vivid quartered oak grain, and carved clawfeet. $1,500

Triple sets of accessory drawers stand tall on this wide princess dresser, housing a single long drawer in the chest supported by carved clawfeet. A carved harp holds the beveled mirror. $1,800

CHESTS, HIGH

The shaped, beveled mirror with carved crest is suspended above the low, bow-front chest of this Princess dresser. $900

Six drawers high, this solid quartersawn chest displays fine grain. It has recessed, paneled sides. A touch of scroll carving accents its fancy board. Ornate brass pulls decorate the drawers. $1,800

An elegant oval beveled mirror is suspended by its harp over the triple serpentined chest of this princess dresser. $900

A center carved crest and scrolled carved ends of the fancy board dress up this straight front, five-drawer high chest. $600

Heavy applied carvings are predominant on the fancy board of this two-over-four drawer high chest. The shaped top follows the lines of the two swelled top drawers. $900

A scroll carved fancy board stands to the rear at the top as a finishing touch in the absence of a mirror and adds to the style of this two over four drawer high chest. The shaped top follows the slight double swell of the two top drawers, further trimmed by scroll carvings on each side of the posts. The shaped and slightly scrolled skirt and legs enhance the bottom. $700

The slightly serpentined face of this high chest is enhanced by a shaped beveled mirror, suspended in its scroll carved harp. The curves of the skirt accent the carved clawfeet. $900 dresser, $1,200 chest.

The carved bonnet box door is centered between pairs of small drawers on each side. Two side-by-side drawers are above, with three full-width, carved drawers below. The shaped fancy board, with carving and finials, crowns this chest. $2,500

Double hat boxes meet in the center above the slightly swelled graduated drawers of this high chest. The large, oval, beveled mirror rest between S-curved supports decorated with applied scroll carvings. $1,500

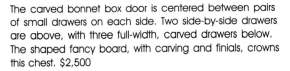

This Eastlake style high chest contains five grooved and incised carved drawers with a variety of flower and leaf patterns. The top is accented with a twisted brass railing. Owl faces appear on the brass drawer pulls. $1,200

Mirrored high chest, matching the Eastlake high chest. The mirror stands tall above the chest with a grooved, scalloped, and decorated harp. $1,500

The swelled bonnet box and double drawers protrude above four full width drawers. Scroll carving under the protrusion to the top drawer accentuates the design. The beveled mirror with carved crest and harp, the decorated sideposts, carved skirt and delicate legs enhance this chest. $1,500

The slightly swelled front of this high chest is complimented by its curved sides, elegantly shaped beveled mirror, rounded sideposts and shaped feet. $1,800

Double offset bonnet boxes with their carved doors are placed with smaller drawers in an interesting design above three full width drawers. The applied scrolls on the fancy board, the shaped sideposts, and the scrolled carving along the skirt add to its character. $1,800

The graceful, slightly bowed front of this high chest contains two-over-five drawers of graduated sizes. The shaped, beveled mirror rests in its decorated harp. The double top follows the bow. Rounded sideposts, carved skirt, and shaped legs enhance its style. $1,800

Quartered oak veneer swirls on the face of this serpentined high bonnet chest as the oval mirror rest in its open harp. Shaped sideposts glide to the shaped clawfooted legs. $1,500

Double offset bonnet boxes scroll carved doors decorate the face of this straight front high chest. The shaped mirror with its carved crest and harp stand above the bowed top. A touch of carving on the skirt finishes the bottom. $1,600

The large, oval, beveled mirror rests in its harp above the drop of this serpentined high chest. 74" tall x 41" wide x 20" deep, this chest offers wide, deep drawers along with two small drawers. $2,100

Bombayed sides with applied scroll carved trimmings enhance the triple serpentined face of this six drawer high chest. The shaped, beveled mirror stands tall above the chest with its carved harp and crest. $2,000

A board center curve swells between two more abrupt curves on the face of this 42" triple serpentined high chest. Double hatboxes create the drop center framing and supporting the harp holding the shaped, beveled mirror with its scroll crest at 72" in height. $2,400

This outstanding high chest displays its tall, intricate gallery and mirrored hatbox above its carved face. The large, carved panel with its brass trimming drops to provide the writing surface for the desk interior enclosed. Three deep drawers are provided below. $2,800

Raised panels and heavy rope-twists decorate this
massive butlers high chest. The door on the left encloses
the hatbox while the door to the right drops down to form
the writing surface for the enclosed desk. Scroll carvings
and rope-twists decorate the mirror harp and frame.
$2,700

WASHSTANDS

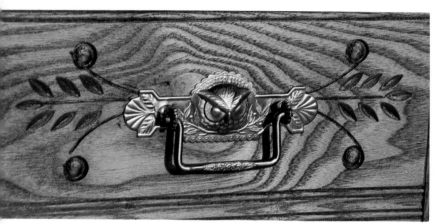

Large, incised daisies decorate the cupboard door with
incised leaf patterns and bull's eyes on the splashboard
and drawers. Owl brasses highlight the face of this
Eastlake style washstand. $900

A scroll-carved crest with a small half-roll decorates this otherwise plain, mirrored washstand. The lines are simple, but appealing. $900

Incised, straight-line carvings decorate the front and scalloped splash board of this Eastlake style washstand. $900

Scrolled carving accentuates the roll crowning the harp supporting the domed, beveled mirror on this large washstand. The case includes contoured drawer fronts decorated with scroll carving depicting open-mouthed lion heads. The round pilasters rest on carved clawfeet. $1,500

This double serpentined washstand displays quartered veneer on the face of its double drawers and cupboard doors. $750

Simply styled, this washstand has a bowed top drawer protruding over double doors. A shaped towel bar awaits the linens. $600

Fluted sideposts and cabriole ball and clawfooted legs are stylish on this quartered oak washstand. The cylinder shaped drawer and rope-twisted trim along the lower edge also add interest. This washstand was to be used as a dining room server. $700

Groove work and incised carvings decorate the splashboard, pilasters, drawer fronts, cupboard door and baseboard of this Eastlake style washstand. $850

Incised sheafs of wheat accent the splashboard while swirled leaf patterns decorate the front of the Eastlake washstand. The groove work and beveled edge along the top demonstrate detailed cabinetwork. Strong mortise and tenon joints, sometimes called "doweled and pinned", also are often found on Eastlake styles. It is a method of jointing, not usually found on later styles within the Oak Period. $850

The raised panel doors add character to this undecorated washstand. The square cut splashboard and top are softened by tapered pilasters and a slightly protruding top drawer. Stamped brass drawer pulls help to dress it up. $650

The geometric lines of Eastlake are predominant on this Eastlake-style washstand. The square, beveled mirror pivots in its enclosed harp above the incised splashboard and below the molded crest. Incised patterns also decorate the drawer fronts and double cupboard doors provided for storage below. $1,200

Curves and carving stand 57" tall on the towel bar of this 35" wide washstand. The shaped top drawer protrudes, adding interest to the face. Scroll carving on the skirt accents between short shaped legs resting on castors. $800

HOTEL WASHSTANDS

A combination dresser and washstand, known as a hotel washstand, was designed to conserve space. Its straight front with a shaped and beveled mirror and harp flow to join the towel bar above the stepped-down case. $1,400

The design for this hotel washstand resembles a small dresser but also includes a cupboard for the chamber pot and a towel bar for the linens, necessary accommodations in the early 1900s. The shaped, beveled mirror, harp and towel bar are decorated with touches of scroll carving which soften the otherwise straight lines. $850

This low princess dresser-washstand combination is dressed up with a shaped, scroll-carved, beveled mirror, a harp, and a towel bar. $900

This stepped-down hotel washstand displays a tall, enclosed, beveled mirror decorated sparingly at the crest with small scrolls. The top protrudes over straight-front drawers and a tiny cupboard is provided on the lower right. Stamped brass pulls accent the drawers. $1,200

ARMOIRES, CHIFFEROBES

Standing tall with its elaborate carved crest at 8 feet, 3 inches, this 58" wide armoire displays shaped and decorated door frames. The original shipping label remains intact from Marstal Furniture Co., Henderdon, KY shipped to Norristown, PA. $2,500

Undecorated, this oak wardrobe provided the utilitarian function of a closet. This one became a pantry cupboard. $950

This 48" wide armoire is decorated only by its center scroll-carved crest. $2,100

Shaped legs support this chifferobe which has a hatbox and five drawers beside a full length, open-grained door. $950

Wide open oak grain travels the door frames and inset panels of this tall armoire. Graceful scrolls decorate the crown and accent the double drawered base. $2,200

Carved clawfeet accent this 44" wide x 68" tall x 21" deep chifferobe. Seven quartered oak drawers and the hatbox compliment the roomy closet, giving wonderful storage. $2,200

A single door with beveled mirror dominates this armoire above a single drawer. Vertical rolls with brass cuffs are set on the corners rising into finials on each side of the shaped carved crest. $1,650

Shaped beveled mirrors reflect the room in the double doors of this armoire. The scroll carved crown enhances the molded top with its center scroll carved decoration as fluted half-columns soften the square corners. Double drawers are provided in the base. $3,200

SHAVING STANDS

DESK CHAIRS

Double pressed swivel desk chair has inverted matched pressings on its two broad back panels with seven turned spindles combining them. Bentwood arms flow from the turned backposts curling under to meet the seat and are supported by three turned spindles. $850

Center left:
Bentwood arrowback swivel desk chair has a tall, carved headpiece with continuous bent backpost arms supported by four large turned spindles. The sculptured saddle seat provides comfort. *Johnson Chair* is embossed on the spring mechanism. $850

Center right:
Tall Bentwood arrowback desk chair has an upholstered headrest with long tapering slats to the upholstered seat. Backposts bend and curl to shape the arms supported by two spindles and reinforcing rods to hold them securely in place. The shapely base has ribbed trim and incised carving decorates the legs. $700

Bottom:
Scrolls and beading decorate the broad headpiece of this swivel desk chair. Eight arrowback spindles provide support as do the backposts as they extend from behind the back, bending to form the arms. Four large, turned spindles provide support. $750

Bowed arms are supported by large turned arm... $650

Center row, left to right:
Elegant quartered oak swivel chair shows its grain on the broad headpiece, center back panel and solid sculptured seat. The curved arms with carved knuckles rest upon shapely arm supports. The legs are neatly designed and flow softly to the floor. Signed *Johnson Chair Co.* on its spring mechanism. $650

Plain quartered oak slat back swivel desk chair with cane seat. $450

A shapely pressed headpiece adorns this spindled swivel desk chair. Bent sideposts curl to the solid seat, shaping the arms supported by three turned spindles. $750

Turned finials frame the pressed headpiece of this spindled swivel desk chair. Shaped arms are supported by three turned spindles and larger turned armposts. $600

Bottom row, left to right:
Beautifully embossed arrowback swivel desk chair. Tall finials frame the headpiece. Bentwood arms, supported by two turned spindles, curl to the saddle seat. $850

A beautifully, deeply carved headpiece crowns this swivel desk chair. Seven turned spindles support the crest as do the turned backposts. Softly rounded arms roll at the ends as they are supported by five turned spindles. The solid seat is deeply sculptured for comfort and has a shapely skirt. $650

The broad headpiece of this elm swivel desk chair is deeply embossed on the outer edges following its shapely lines. Two decorated slats extend to the solid seat on each side of seven straight, thin slats. Wide curving arms are supported by four large, turned spindles. $650

Undecorated solid seated slat-back swivel desk chair. $400

This outstanding swivel desk chair displays a carved ram's head on its quarter-sawn headpiece. Beautifully turned sideposts support the crest as do eight turned spindles connected to the carved lower back panel. Shapely arms are supported by four turned spindles and larger armpost as they form a deep seat. $950

ARM
CHAIRS

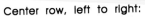

Center row, left to right:
A shapely, pressed headpiece decorates this swivel desk chair. Long, turned spindles, turned sideposts, and bent arms frame the solid seat. $750

ARMCHAIRS

This armchair sets off its shaped crest and broad center back panel with its curled arms, shaped saddle seat, turned legs, and double front rungs. $350

The scrolled quarter sawn crest of this shapely armchair flows into the arm rest, then radically curves in reverse to shape its own supports. The large caned seat sets above gracefully shaped legs joined by concave stretchers connected by shaped rungs. $375

Bottom row, left to right:
The continuous bent arms of this chair flow gracefully from the back as they are supported by shaped and curled armposts. Shaped spindles fit the occupant as does the sculptured seat. Cabriole legs braced by concave stretchers add to the elegance. $450

The caned back lightens the look of this simply designed armchair. The shaped seat rests on straight legs as the side stretchers curve to meet the back legs. $250

Straight horizontal lines carry through on this pair of armchair. Two horizontal slats support the back below the wide top rails. The arms extend and bend to the solid boxed seat which rests on slightly flared legs. $450 pair.

Top right:
Quartered oak grain glows on the round back and sculptured seat of this office armchair. Often used as *jury chairs*, the construction allows comfort for its occupant due to its contouring. The straight legs rest squarely on the floor. $950 set of four.

Bottom right:
Thirteen spiral spindles support the round back of this decorative armchair. The shaped solid seat is wide and comfortable, resting upon the spool turned legs. $550

DESKS, ROLL TOP

This 48"-high, raised panel, S-roll-top desk has a basic design of classic style. It has been preserved with its original, swivel desk chair. $3,700

A 48"-high, S-roll-top desk contains a nice, slotted interior. The center originally held a typewriter that could be flipped up for use. The drawers have raised panels with plain pulls. $3,300

This 48"-high, low, S-roll desk has recessed panel sides and tall legs. $1,800

This single pedestal, rolltop desk is supported to the left by turned legs. The high S-roll is attractive as it conceals its interior and writing surface. The original finish remains. The keyhole escutcheon reads "Corbin Cabinet Lock Co., Patented December 16, '84." Collection of Robert and Lisa Stull. $3,200

The elaborate interior of this 60" rolltop and its high, S-roll are outstanding. $6,500

A 59"-high, S-roll-Top desk has an elaborate interior with drawers and cubby holes. Vertical and horizontal raised panels construct the desk on all sides. Raised paneled drawers with shell-carved drawer pulls enhance the front. $4,900

A high, S-roll is featured on this 50" rolltop desk with recessed panel construction and shell-carved drawer pulls. $3,300

DESKS, FLAT TOP

This 48"-wide flat top, office desk has an inlaid burled wood top with vertical recessed paneled sides. Four drawers on the right side and two drawers and a hinged cupboard with pigeonholes on the left are arranged with pullout writing tablets on both sides. $1,400

Outstanding, solid quartered oak is beautiful in this 60"-wide, office desk. Shell-carved drawer pulls enhance the wide, raised-paneled drawer fronts. $2,500

Elaborately carved, this desk displays intricate scrolls on the molded top and has three drawers in the apron. Each pedestal, containing three drawers, rests on huge, curved, claw feet. The back side of each pedestal has false drawers. Each end bears a framed portrait of the legendary character "Northwind." $8,500

This 48"-wide, solid quartered-oak, flat-top desk is shown disassembled. When assembled, the two pedestals are joined in the center by a connecting brace which is laying on the right pedestal. The top is secured with screws. This desk has four drawers and a pullout writing tablet on the left with a single drawer cupboard with pigeon holes on the right. Not visible is a concealed cupboard on the right side to store confidential documents. $1,200

The swivel office chair has a comfortable, shaped back and a solid, reinforced seat. $500

This single pedestal, flat-top desk has a single set of four drawers on the left. The end panels and back are distinctive with vertical raised panels. $1,100

Quartered oak veneer decorates this partners', flat-top desk. Two small drawers and a cupboard on each side provide a minimum storage area. Carved ball and claw feet conform with the rounded corners to support the desk. $1,350

In solid, quarter-sawn oak with vivid grain, this 36" wide x 26" deep single pedestal desk is truly outstanding. Raised panels and shaped drawer pulls add to its vibrant beauty. An oak rail is provided at the back to enhance the desk top. A name plate is mounted on the back...actually its face. $1,500

FILING CABINETS

Beautiful quartered oak was chosen for the recessed side panels and face of this four-drawer, standard size, filing cabinet. The sculptured top and shaped brass drawer markers are attractive additions. $1,050

This quartered oak, legal-size file cabinet has double card file drawers above and three file drawers below. $1,000

Straight lines, recessed panels, and quartered oak construct this well-made four-drawer filing cabinet. $950

This cabinet offers storage with style within its recessed panel, quartered oak door. $900

Top row, left to right:
This document file stands tall as its cambered door rolls down, revealing shelves for various forms to be filed. $1,200

This combination filing unit by Library Bureau Solemakers includes a bookcase with sliding, glass-doors, two standard-size filing drawers, and a large, enclosed storage cabinet. Organization plus! $1,800

Forty-four various sized drawers offer organizational possibilities, 40" wide x 62" high. $1,900

Center row, left to right:
Four, 4" x 6" card file drawers have quartered oak drawer faces in a straight-grained cabinet. A name plate is marked "The Advance Card Index Cabinet." $225

This stacked unit includes 18 card file drawers in three sections, each set upon the other, and supported by a straight-legged base. $1,200

Legal size filing drawers are housed within this "Library Bureau Solemakers" filing cabinet. Recessed panels formed by the structural stiles and cross rails enhance the sides and back. Original brass hardware shines on the quarter-sawn drawer faces. $975

Bottom row, left:
This card file bears an insignia upon its drawer pull reading "Labor Saving Device." The dove-tailed case is 10" wide x 15½" deep x 7" high to house 4" x 8" cards. The original finish remains as does the originators or owners label reading "Wm. H. Hoskins Co., Philadelphia, Pa." $150

Opposite page, center right:
Four, 3" x 5" card file drawers are housed in this quartered oak cabinet. $250

Lady's Work Room

SEWING RELATED

This Singer sewing machine is housed in an oak case. The lid folds to the left to enable the machine head to be lifted into position. Double drawers are for attachments and notions. The cast iron base bears the SINGER name above the treadle. $375

Manufactured by "The Illinois Sewing Machine Co. of Rockford, Illinois," this "New Royal" model was of the utmost quality and convenience. Offered in the 1917/1918 Larkin catalog as No. C1024, it was described as "the most desirable of Sewing Machines." No expense was spared to make it so. It was "the 6-drawer drop-head style with center movable panel." All woodwork was of the finest quarter-sawn oak. The handsome French-leg stand bears the name "New Royal" on the treadle. A special automatic device lifted the sewing head automatically into position and unlocked the drawers. When closed, the head dropped into its receptacle and the drawers automatically locked; no key was required. $48 worth of Larkin purchase or coupons were required to obtain this model which was guaranteed for 25 years. It was shipped to its owner directly from the factory. Collection of Douglas and Virginia Donnolo. $500 in immaculate original condition.

Shown in the 1912 Larkin catalog as the "Chautauqua Sewing Desk No. 25", this piece was described as a "compact and convenient receptacle for materials and all accessories under lock and key." The top, when extended, was 23½" x 48", with the extension and supporting legs folding under to reduce the size to 24" square. $650

The desk shown folded displays its original plain drawer pulls and stretchers. The extended desk (as shown) has been dressed up with fancier pulls and escutcheons. Today, many such serving desks serve as end tables since the 25" height is ideal. $700

VANITIES

Cantilever mirrors enhance the straight lines of this vibrantly grained quartered oak veneered vanity. $700 pedestal, see page 72

Vertical serpentined drawers flank the beveled mirror of this vanity which is supported by thin, tapered legs. $1,350 stool, see introduction.

The oval mirror of this vanity has a carved crest. The vanity table has a shaped quarter-sawn veneer top with a single drawer, beaded trim, and four shaped legs. Dated 1905 underneath the drawer. The co-ordinated chair is reflected in the mirror. Notice the lines of the chair leg are similar to the vanity leg. $1,200

A round, beveled mirror rests in a shaped harp over this vanity. The irregularly shaped top is supported by legs of uncharacteristic shape. $750

An oval beveled mirror hangs over the quarter-sawn veneer top and the double drawers of this vanity supported by shaped legs with tiny clawfeet. 5'6" high x 34½" wide x 19¼" deep. $1,200 chair, see page 176 top right.

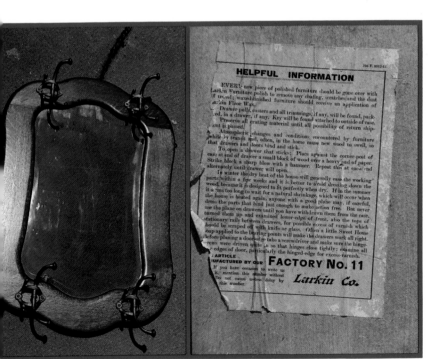

This "Larkin Hanging Hat Rack NO. 85" has a "heavy shaped frame of selected Quarter-sawed Oak...Has four brass-plated two way hooks of rich design...Rack is 33½ in. long and 23½ in. wide" (as described in the 1908 Larkin catalog). The original label remains intact, reading: "Factory No. 11 Larkin Co." $400

Top row, left to right:
Rope-twists are applied to the frame's sides and end turnings of this solid, quarter-sawn, rectangular, beveled mirror. $450

The square, beveled mirror, set on its point, rests within a frame with decorative molding, large carvings, and brass hat hooks on the corners. $475

An oval mirror rests in a quarter-sawn frame with double hooks mounted on rounded corners to create this hat rack. $450

Center right:
"Stick 'n ball" turnings with bentwood accents frame the square, beveled mirror of this hat rack. $350

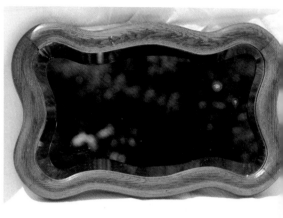

Top row, left to right:
This curved and beveled mirror reflects the graceful lines of an adjacent washstand as the mirror sits on the floor. $300

An eight-inch-round, carved face smiles between "stick 'n ball" turned spindles above the wide bevel of its mirror. 26" high by 20" wide, the incised frame includes brass hat hooks. $450

10"-wide x 18"-high, this small, beveled mirror was probably hung originally on a narrow, serpentined high-chest. $125

Center row, left to right:
Outstanding scrolls ornament the 7"-deep carved frame of this 23½" x 29½" mirror with a one-inch bevel. $700

Outstanding in its detail, this hat rack mirror is intricate in its style. Stick 'n ball decorates the top as open rope-twists and turnings decorate the side supports. The center beveled mirror falls forward, suspended by small chains to provide better viewing. Hat holders pivot outward to accomodate hats as shaped pegs pivot forward to accomodate ties. They can be returned to the wall when not in use. 31" wide x 27" tall. $600

FERN STANDS

A claw-footed platform supports the turned column of this pedestal. $400

The turned column of this pedestal rests on a square base. $375

Center row, left to right:
Tall and tapered, this stand, in a A-frame design, has additional use with its four shelves. It is signed "Miller Cabinet Co., No. 1122, Rochester, N.Y." $400

Four legs with ball and claw feet support the fine, spiral-twist column and a 17"-diameter top on this 33"-tall candle stand. One of a matched pair. $650 pair.

STOOLS

Opposite page, left to right:
This tapered, turned pedestal displays its highly figured, solid, quarter-sawn wood on its top. $375

The tapered, fluted pedestal with pineapple ball is beautifully designed. $475

This pedestal is attractively turned. $225

Top row, left to right:
Doubled turned on an octagon pillar, this pedestal stands 36" tall. Shown in the 1919/1920 Larkin catalog as No. 9020N1, it was "given with $7 purchase of Products or for $7 in Coupons." $375

This pedestal is turned and elegantly fluted. $375

A pedestal which displays a turned and fluted column. $450

Rope-twisted trim details the hinged leather upholstered seat which encloses shoe-shine equipment. Somewhat elaborate for a shoe-shine stool, it sits upon large scaled clawfeet in addition to its incised circle carvings and decorated, raised panels on each side. $375

This classic piano stool has quartered oak grain on the adjustable swivel top. A large, turned center post supports the turned rungs and turned legs rest on glass ball and talon clawfeet. $250

Left:
This organ stool is similar to the piano stool in design with the addition of a back rest. The player applies pressure to the stool's back while pumping the foot pedals of the organ. $425

Above:
This stool, called the "New India Seat" in the 1901 Larkin catalog, was available for one Larkin certificate. Constructed of five-ply veneer with a concave top, it was described as "strongly made, but light and graceful and an ornament to any room." $250

MEDICINE CHESTS

Left to right:
Undecorated except for the scrolled crest, the flat face of this medicine chest displays its beveled mirror. $225

This medicine chest, with a large, beveled mirror door, also provides a shelf at the top and towel bar at the bottom. $375

Rope-twisted trim enhances the beveled mirror of this medicine chest, which also provides a drawer. $350

So sweet in its style, this 21½" tall corner medicine chest displays its incised, carved crest, beveled mirror, and drawer with beaded trim on its 10" face. The 4½" side panels continue the curves at the top as they display grooved detailing. $475

Similar medicine chest, each with a beveled mirror door and drawer. The chest on the right is dressed up with a larger mirror and pressed pattern on the drawer. $300

The molded top with its carved trim accentuates the raised panel doors and two small drawers of this corner wall cabinet. Courtesty of Connie Mohn. $350

ACCENT CHAIRS

Northwind's face is pressed upon the multi-ply seat sets within a molded frame, resting upon tapered flared legs. $375

Puffed cheeks blow from the Northwind face carved at the head of this ornamental chair. A slender quarter-sawn center panel appears to be a long neck as it is flanked by double turned spindles. The shaped quarter sawn seat is supported by tapered legs joined by a curved rung attached to the seat by short spindles. $400

VANITY CHAIRS

Unusually carved, this Mate's chair bears the face of the Captain, scowling with his pipe. The chair may have been constructed and carved to pass the hours aboard ship. The chair is assembled of flat interlocking boards fitted with wedges. It disassembles easily into five pieces, enabling it to be stored flat in a seaman's chest. $400

This plain quartered oak occasional chair bears no decoration other than the shape and pierced design of its tall back. The seat is sculptured resting upon splayed legs. The manufacturer's paper label reads "H.C. Dexter Chair Co., Black River, New York Made in the United States." Shown in its original finish. $225

Northwind shows one of his carved faces within the shapely outline of this chair as he overlooks the rounded carved seat supported by widely splayed, turned legs. $425

This small-scale chair displays gentle, curved lines throughout. $150

The pierced center back panel highlights this small scale chair. The shaped headpiece is supported by tapered, turned single post back legs as the increase in dimensions from the top to the floor to support the chair. Turned, flared legs and turned rungs add further detail. $145

Simply designed, six long spindles support the curved headpiece of this vanity chair. Single post back legs add strength. Turned legs and rungs add interest. $150

Top row, left to right:

Pair of child's chairs signed Thornet Bentwood cane backed and cane seated chairs. 25½" tall with 12½" diameter seats. $475 pair.

Combination chair with elaborately decorated quarter sawn wood. It has a broad carved headpiece and back panel. It has four positions for a high chair, a youth chair, a play table, and (at lowest position) a rocker. $650

Beautifully pressed, carved, and quarter-sawn convertible high chair has a decorated headpiece and a back panel with a left over tray, spindled arm supports, cane seat and turned rungs. $675

Bottom row, left to right:

Convertible pressedback highchair which lowers from its full height to its lowest level as a stroller, or a "chariot" with propelling handle. When in the up position, the handle rests at the back of chair moving into position as the chair is lowered. $650

Simply styled highchair is unadorned. Thirteen tiny straight spindles form the back below a bentwood crest. The legs are noticeably splayed to avoid tipping. Plain in design, but distinctive. $375

Pressedback highchair with a large embossed headpiece reinforced with seven spindles. Single post back and front legs flair at the floor for added stability. The arms are supported by four spindles and larger arm post, which is securely fastened to the seat. The arms in turn support the tray, which lifts over the back to create a youth chair. $600

Top row, left right:

Mission style highchair is incredibly sturdy, with its square legs balanced by the curvature of the single post back legs. The large tray locks down for safety. The shaped seat is comfortable, along with the slat back. $375

This child's pressedback rocking chair displays an oval leaf pressing on its broad quarter-sawn headpiece. Six twisted spindles decorate the back. The turned sideposts, shaped arms, turned legs and rungs, and cane seat add style. $400

This Mission style child's rocker is dressed up with its turned sideposts and arm supports. The shaped solid seat shows its quartered oak grain as it rests on square legs. $350

Original varnish remains in its darkened lack-lustre condition as this highchair displays its deeply embossed headpiece and splat. $600

Bottom row, left to right:

The years have shown their mark by a missing spindle and damaged tray on this convertible highchair. Basically sound and in operating condition. Minor repairs and a new finish will restore beauty and serviceability to the chair as it displays its large embossed headpiece. $750

Arrowback child's rocker shows its light pressings, bentwood arms and solid seat above turned legs. $375

Solid, quarter-sawn oak, raised panels are displayed beautifully in the construction of this 34" wide x 2½" tall by 20" deep child's desk. A 12" lift up extension is provided to offer additional work area along with a pull out writing tablet to the right. The four drawers are enhances by raised panels and shell carved pulls. High quality. $900

Collection of Lisa and
Robert Stull. $475

Incised leaf carvings decorate the drop front and top
shelf of this child's desk which has two bookshelves below
the desk. $500

CHILD'S DESKS

This oak child's desk (35" wide x 18" deep x 26" high) has
straight legs and six shallow drawers. It now serves the
purpose of an end table. $450

This small scale, undecorated, drop front desk is cute in its
simple style. (24" wide, 42" high, and 13½" deep). $450

Restoration

Restoration is the process by which an item is returned to its former or original state.

The process can be capsulized; strip, repair, sand, refinish. Sounds easy, but many hours are involved to complete each step. Only those possessing the patience to experiment will be able to obtain the best result.

First, the purchase. The condition of the chosen item will determine the quantity of time and labor necessary to restore its original beauty. A broken down piece needing many major repairs is hardly a bargain. The savings will vanish in the consumed restoration time. An item in good, basically sound, condition, needing only minor repairs, will give a much greater return for the initial investment. Restoration time will be saved and the finished product will give pleasure much sooner.

Secondly, the preparation. Hardware is removed and placed in a safe spot for later polishing. The beveled mirror or mirrors are removed from their frames to be resilvered if needed. Now you are ready, if you have your tools and supplies ready.

The work begins. The stripping of the old finish is next. The darkened varnish or shellac is removed by the application of chemical "stripper." Applied to the old finish, it will reduce it to a black "goop" after a few minutes. While in this state, the softened finish is removed carefully with a scraper and steel wool pads, revealing the bare wood beneath. Lacquer thinner, a chemical solvent is then used to wipe down the piece to remove all traces of the old finish from carvings and crevices. The key is clean. If it's not...do it again and again until it is clean!

Now, for the repairs. Loosened joints are glued, blemishes touched up. This is where time is saved. A good oak piece will require little at this point.

Sanding is next, the degree of which is determined by the condition of the oak. Fine sandpaper is used always with the grain. The surface should be smooth to the touch with no rough edges.

The staining comes next. What color? That is for you to decide. To enhance the grain, a medium oak stain color will give the best result. Experiments are necessary for the inexperienced to obtain the color desired. The chosen color is applied. A sealing stain works well as it seals the pores of the oak while adding color as it is absorbed. The excess stain is removed. Do you have your color? If not, reapply the stain, allow it to set until the desired color appears. Allow the piece to dry.

The final major step is the finishing. Several coats of clear lacquer in a semi-gloss lustre gives a nice look to the finished piece, but the look desired is again a personal choice.

Finally, the brass hardware is polished and returned to its spot. The resilvered mirror is placed in its frame. Voilá. The restored oak gives beauty and service once again.

Note: These areas of restoration are briefly described. They will not be completed as quickly as you read these paragraphs. If patience is not yours, I would recommend shopping for your oak furniture treasures in a quality restored condition offered by a reputable dealer. The finished product can be seen and inspected. The rewards of its purchase, beauty, and service can be reaped immediately in instant gratification.

T[...]

A

Acanthus leaf—Adapted from the more-or-less ragged leaf of the acanthus plant, a native of Southern Europe. The leaf is the distinguishing mark of the Corinthian capital.

Applied carving—Ornamentation crafted separately, then attached to achieve decoration, as carvings and turnings.

Applied decoration—Ornamentation crafted separately, then attached to a furniture piece, carvings, turnings, etc.

Apron—A narrow strip of designed or plain wood adjoining the base of cabinet bodies, chair seats, table tops, etc., extending between the tops of leg or feet brackets. Often used to conceal underframing.

Arm chair—Compared with the ordinary chair, the arm chair is larger and more conducive to repose. When extended to serve as the "seat of honor," it corresponds in style to the other chairs of the set. It differs only in its size. Mismatched armchairs are often used today to accent and expand a set of side chairs.

Arm support—The vertical or curved upright supporting the front end of chair arms.

Armoire—Synonymous with "wardrobe" as a large cupboard originally used for storing clothes. Often used today as entertainment centers.

Arrowback—Flattened spindles, often bent for comfort, having arrow-pointed end shapes, spaced to form chair backs.

Art Nouveau—The French Arts and Crafts movement. A style of surface ornamentation dominated by pervasive curvilinear, often asymetrical rhythms.

Artificial graining—A method of applying paint to imitate natural graining. Applied to a piece constructed of poplar or elm or on straight grained oak to give the appearance of quarter-sawn wood.

Arts and Crafts Movement—An English aesthetic movement during the latter half of the nineteenth century, marking the beginning of a new appreciation of the decorative arts throughout Europe.

Its idealistic leaders, John Ruskin and William Morris, established the principles upon which the movement was built.

Prior to the harnessing of steam, the world was primarily an agricultural society depending on craftsmen for furniture, decorative arts and accessories. By the 1850s, mass production saw the men, women and the young people toiling in the factories turning out inferior products.

Morris and his followers were dismayed by the plight of the working class and the results of machine workmanship. They stressed pride in hand-crafted articles. They believed that by raising the status of the craftsmen, they would also increase the quality of the items produced.

Guilds were established in which t[...] could work under ideal conditions sellin[...] the English public.

The influence of these men spread to [...] States in the late 1880s. The English provide[...] for the Arts and Crafts philosophy. The [...] popularized it.

Atlas—A supporting pillar designed in the sh[...] man. The female version is a caryatid.

B

Ball foot—A ball termination of a leg, usually turne[...]

Baluster—A small, slender turned column.

Bead—A small molding of a nearly semi-circular section.

Bed—An article of furniture upon which one rests or sleeps.

Bedroom suite—The basic set consisted of a high-back bed with its footboard often called "bedstead" at the time, a dresser for the storage of clothing and a washstand as a place to "wash up." Inside bathrooms existed only in the city.

Bench—An elongated seat, usually intended for several persons, furnished with a back and arms.

Bentwood—A method developed in 1836 by German cabinetmaker Michael Thonet, when he perfected the method of soaking stacks of thin veneer in hot glue to render the wood pliable enough to be molded into bent forms.

Beveled—An edge cut to an angle other than 90°; the inclination which one surface makes with another when not at right angles.

Bombé—An outward swelling, curving, or bulging.

Boss—A round, applied decoration, sometimes with inscribed circles or a raised turning.

Boxed Seat—A form of chair construction showing an apron-like structure beneath the seat that connects the legs, thus "boxing the seat" and strengthening the chair. Often combined with H-rungs set lower on the legs.

Braces—Short bentwood supports attached to the back leg and seat where they meet to provide strength. Found often on pressed back chairs with single post back legs. Also known as "hiphuggers."

Buffet—A small cupboard or counter for refreshments.

Bulbous—Having the shape of a bulb. Often used to describe a large, bulging table leg.

Bun foot—A flattened ball or bun shape with slender ankle above.

Burled—A distorted grain pattern produced by a flattened hemispherical outgrowth on a tree, called a burl, from which veneer is made.

C

Cabriole—A term applied to legs that swell outward at the upper part or knee and inward at the lower part or ankle. There are many variations with different feet.

Cane—Long, narrow strips of rattan used for the weaving of chair seats and backs. The strips can be woven by hand through holes located around an open seat, or the cane can be obtained in factory woven sheets and then applied to the seat by means of a spline fitting into a groove. Both methods were and continue to be used.

Cane chair—Where the seat alone or in conjunction with the back is of woven or pressed cane-work.

Cantilever mirrors—Triple mirrors mounted in such a way that the two outside mirrors are attached by hinges on one side only to allow adjustment toward the center.

Capital—The top of a column.

Cartouche—A decorative device based upon the unrolled scroll.

Caryatid—A supporting pillar designed in the form of a female. Sometimes the whole length of the figure is employed, sometimes only the upper half. The male version is called *Atlas*.

Cased—Any cabinet-type item of furniture.

Castors—Small wheels set into the feet or base of furniture to allow easier movement. Wood, metal, or glass can be used.

Chamfer—An edge cut off to form a slanting surface, leaving a raised panel.

Cheval mirror—A decorative mirror suspended in a free-standing upright frame, usually made to pivot for maximum visibility. Usually used for dressing.

Chifferobe—A piece of furniture designed with a closet on one side and a chest of drawers on the other. The combination is sometimes enclosed by double doors enclosing both areas.

Chiffonier—A tall, narrow chest of drawers, often referred to as a *highboy*.

Chimera—A fire-breathing creature, originating in Greek mythology and having a lion's head, goat's body, and serpent's tail. It is generally a horrible creature of the imagination.

China cabinet—A glass enclosed article of furniture designed to house and display glass and dinnerware.

Circa—Around the time of, as circa 1900. Abbreviation is ca.

Claw and ball feet—The foot of a leg shaped as a 3-toed talon claw as it envelopes a ball. Seen as metal claws over a crystal glass ball or as carved claw and ball completely of wood.

Clawfoot—The foot of a leg carved in the shape of a lion's paw or sometimes a bear claw. Can be found on all furniture items standing on legs.

Concave—Curving inwardly; opposite of convex.

Concave seat—Or "dropped seat", where the middle and front of which are lower than the sides.

Convex—Curving outwardly; opposite of concave.

Cornice—The horizontal molding found at the top on furniture.

Crest—The top-most decorative ornament on a piece of furniture. The ornamental peak.

Cross-rail—A horizontal bar in a chair back.

Cupboard—An item of furniture having an enclosed storage area. Often the top is enclosed by glass doors with the base cabinet enclosed by solid doors. A closed cupboard has solid doors enclosing both areas.

Curio cabinet—A small scale, glass-enclosed article of furniture to house and display a prized collection. Often constructed with a mirrored back and crystal shelves, allowing vertical light penetration.

Cylinder chest—A cabinet with many shallow drawers, designed exclusively for the storage of phonograph cylinders. The phonograph sat on the top.

Cylinder roll—A solid, curved, sliding top concealing the writing surface or storage area found on secretary desks. Self storing, it rolls back into the desk. Often called a *barrel roll*.

D

Day bed—A sofa or couch, usually not placed in the bedroom, upon which one rests or naps during the day.

Decoration—The process of applying various elements to beautify objects.

Dished seat—A solid seat with a slight round indentation.

Dolphin—A marine animal whose head and body, or head alone, is often used for decorative purposes.

Dovetailing—Mortise and tendon joints in furniture construction where the mortise flares resembling a dove's tail.

Drop front—As found on a desk being a hinged lid dropping forward to form a writing surface on the underside.

E

Eastlake, Charles Locke (1836-1906)—An English architect interested in exterior design and furniture. He introduced furniture designs in total rebellion against the fancy English Victorian styles. His design possessed simplicity in rectangular shapes. He felt that curves wasted wood and lacked comfort. Eastlake's designs were to be clean, practical, and functional, with old gothic ornamentation and burled walnut trim added to some.

Following a favorable exhibition of Eastlake's new furniture designs at the Philadelphia Exposition in 1876, American manufacturers expanded his design to their own interpretations. Incised lines and carvings were added in "Butterprint" flower, leaf and vine patterns. This was not the style Eastlake advocated, but it is known by his name. The style remained popular until about 1890.

Eastlake-style—See Charles Eastlake.

Eclectic—Combining designs and styles from various periods to produce a distinctive blend.

Elements of Decoration—These are geometrical lines, ornament, natural foliage, artificial objects, animal and the human figure.

Embellish—To enhance beauty with additional decoration.

Escutcheon—A shaped plate or brass fitting for a keyhole.

Expositions—Similar to World Fairs, Expositions were actually on-going exhibitions. They provided a means for the furniture designers to introduce their new ideas to the public, thereby gaining acceptance. The Grand Rapids, Michigan Furniture Exposition launched the acceptance of Mission styling. The Paris Exposition

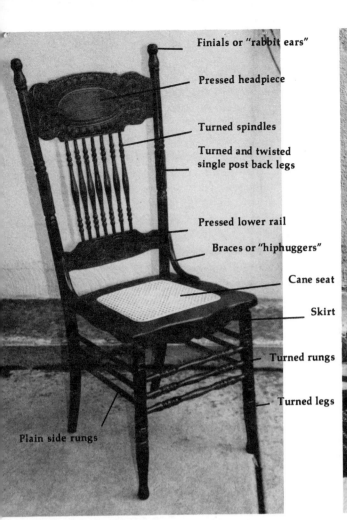

Finials or "rabbit ears"

Pressed headpiece

Turned spindles

Turned and twisted
single post back legs

Pressed lower rail

Braces or "hiphuggers"

Cane seat

Skirt

Turned rungs

Turned legs

Plain side rungs

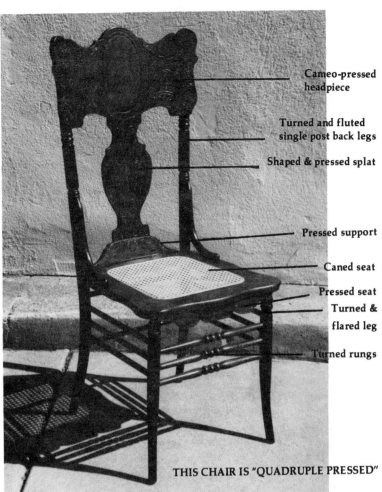

Cameo-pressed
headpiece

Turned and fluted
single post back legs

Shaped & pressed splat

Pressed support

Caned seat

Pressed seat

Turned &
flared leg

Turned rungs

THIS CHAIR IS "QUADRUPLE PRESSED"

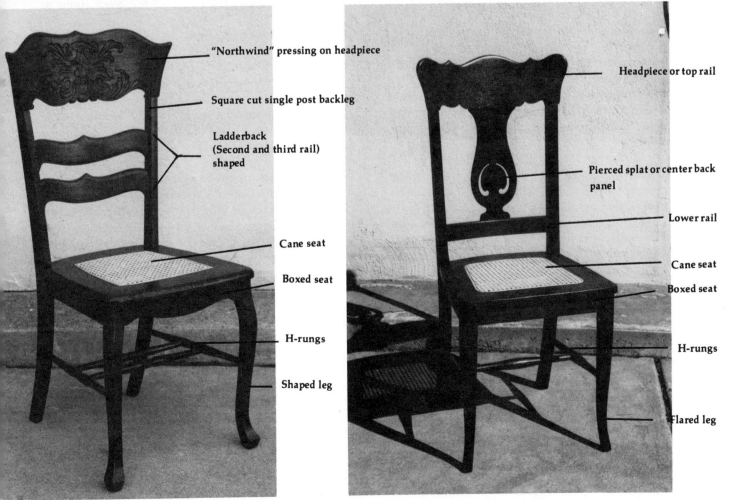

"Northwind" pressing on headpiece

Square cut single post backleg

Ladderback
(Second and third rail)
shaped

Cane seat

Boxed seat

H-rungs

Shaped leg

Headpiece or top rail

Pierced splat or center back
panel

Lower rail

Cane seat

Boxed seat

H-rungs

Flared leg

initiated the acceptance of "Art Nouveau."

Extension table—A dining table constructed with slides to expand its size as needed to accomodate additional leaves.

F

Fancy Board—A decorative finishing board used on a furniture item that does not have a mirror, such as a buffet or high chest; similar to a splashboard on a washstand.

Fern stand—An item of furniture having a center column supporting the top on which a flowing plant is placed for display.

Finger-grip—Openings for the hand, made in wooden backs, for convenience in moving.

Finial—A decorative finishing device for any sort of projecting upright, often called "rabbit ears" when found on the uprights of chairs.

Fleur-de-lis—A conventionalized flower used in decoration.

Fluting—Channelings. The object is to give animation to a smooth shaft. Opposite of reeding.

Fretwork—Interlaced ornamental work, sometimes perforated and sometimes applied on solid backgrounds.

G

Gadroon—A carved molding used mainly on table tops and chair edges.

Gallery—A decorative railing around the tops of furniture.

Gargoyle—A grotesquely carved creature used as an ornament.

Gingerbread—Excessive ornamentation producing a showy appearance.

Griffin—A chimerical beast having the union of a lion's body with the head and wings of an eagle. The fore extremities may belong to either the lion or the eagle.

Grotesque—Fantastic, often incredibly ugly, monsters produced by the combination of human, animal, and plant organisms.

H

H-rungs—A design of strengthening rungs attaching the front legs to the back, with a center rung that attaches these to each other across the middle, forming an "H".

Half-figures—Popular as startings for ornaments, the upper body undergoes little variation from its natural form. Below the breast or stomach, the scroll ornament grows.

Hardware—Metal used on a piece of furniture. Drawer pulls, hinges, screws, nails. Often used as "original hardware intact"—meaning that nothing has been replaced.

Harp—The structure supporting a mirror or dresser or high chest.

Headpiece—Top-most rail of a chair, plain or fancy.

Highboy—A tall chest of drawers in two sections, the base on tall legs.

Knee—The uppermost part of a cabriole leg.

L

Ladderback—A chair-back in which a series of horizontal cross rails were used instead of a splat, giving the effect of a ladder.

Laminating—The process involving the steam heating under pressure of 4 to 16 layers of wood to produce greater strength.

Larkin Soap Company—John D. Larkin, born in 1845, in Buffalo, New York, went to work for Weller's Buffalo soap factory at the age of 16. The company moved to Chicago in 1870 where Larkin became a partner in 1871. John sold his interest in 1875, returned to Buffalo, and set up his own soap business. He first manufactured a type of yellow soap named "Sweet Home Soap."

Larkin sold his soap through retailers from 1875 to 1885. He then devised a system that revolutionized his industry. He began selling directly to the consumer in 1885, eliminating the various middlemen expenses. The savings was passed on to the customer by offering "free premiums", equal in value to the price of the product. The popular "Larkin Pressedback" dining chair was given for $10.00 worth of Larkin products.

By 1892, the company became the Larkin Soap Manufacturing Company. Elbert Hubbard, Larkin's founding secretary and treasurer, also Larkin's brother-in-law, was a skilled advertising agent who helped develop the "Larkin Club" for housewives, their relatives, and friends. By joining the "Larkin Club", housewives could earn delightful premiums in exchange for purchases. This created an incentive to become a loyal Larkin customer. Certificates given for products purchased could be accumulated and redeemed for lovely items to beautify the home.

The Larkin idea grew rapidly. The 1905 catalog featured 116 products; the 1912 catalog offered 550 products with seven Larkin branch locations. Buffalo, New York was the manufacturing location for Larkin furniture.

John D. Larkin died on February 15, 1926. His work was carried forward until the company suffered hard times during the late 1930s. The company was liquidated in 1941.

There is no monument to express recognition of the industry that put Buffalo on the map. Frank Lloyd Wright designed the Administration building, one of the largest in the world at the time, housing 1800 employees; it was demolished in 1950. The main factory building now sits anonymously.

However, "Larkin Oak" remains as a tribute. It is actively sought and collected today as it was a century ago; in itself, a tribute to John D. Larkin and his Larkin Soap Company.

Loveseat—A settee designed for two persons.

Lyre—A decorative motif, selected from the musical instrument of the same name.

M

Masque—The French word combing "masks" and "caricatures" to describe countenances. The former being the delineations of beautiful faces and the latter being faces grinning, deformed or distorted by accessories or terminating in foliage. Masks and caricatures pass into each other as clearly expressed by this one word.

Mission furniture—The generic term used to describe all the solid, plain, straight-lined oak furniture of strong construction that was manufactured during the early years of the twentieth century. Many companies produced this style, reflecting various levels of quality. One of the distinguishing features between quality Arts and Crafts Mission furniture and mediocre Mission-style copies is the presence of quarter-sawn oak lumber and pegged joints, found in the former.

Molding—A frame or border constructed by shaped lengths of wood.

Morris, William (1834-1896)—An English reformer, poet and interior designer became profoundly disturbed by the deterioration of style, craftsmanship and public taste as a result of the industrial revolution. He advocated the return to excellence in craftsmanship.

Morris and his followers disliked the overly ornate home interiors, with their eclectic furniture designs. They advocated furniture with cleaner, plainer lines. The style did not sell well in England. However, his simple designs sowed the seeds for the Arts and Crafts movement which flourished from 1882 until 1914.

Best known for his invention of the reclining chair, William Morris found Victorian chairs to be most uncomfortable. About 1860, he designed an "easy chair" with thick cushions and an adjustable back. An iron rod rested in a slotted bracket supporting the hinged chairback. Placed in the desired groove, the occupant could "recline" at any one of three or four angles. The reclining armchair is known as the "Morris chair." The style was manufactured in America by the thousands. Some are absolutely plain, while others are elaborately decorated with turned spindles, and carved decoration.

Mortise and tenon—A mortise is a hole or slot in a piece of wood. A tenon is a prong or protruding tongue in another piece of wood. The tenon fits snugly into the mortise to form a tight joint.

Motif—The controlling idea manifested in a work or any part of a work. The dominant feature.

Music cabinet—An enclosed item of furniture designed for storage of musical supplies; sheet music, player piano rolls, phonograph records, cylinders, etc.

N

Northwind—A grotesque mask, depicting the ugly and bizarre. The use of the mask as an ingredient of decoration dates to ancient Greek and Roman times.

O

Ornamentation—Details added to heighten attractiveness.

P

Pier Mirror—A tall, narrow mirror originally used in a foyer or between two windows.

Pierced—To have cut-out areas incorporated in the design as a pierced splat-back on a chair. Also carved backs with opening within the carved design.

Pilaster—A flat column attached to the face of a plain surface mainly as a ornamental support for an arch, cornice, or other superstructure.

Pressedback—A decorative design embossed most often on the backs of chairs. The pattern was produced by first steam heating the wood to soften its texture and then pressing the design into the wood with a steel die. Pressed patterns are also seen on the aprons of parlor and dining tables.

Q

Quarter-sawn—Lumber taken from the log by first cutting it into four pie-shaped wedges. Each wedge is sliced radially to expose the pith rays running from the center outward, creating a two-tone pattern with curved grain. Furniture of the best quality is quarter-sawn, which preserves strength and minimizes warping. More expensive than straight-sawn, as quarter-sawing wastes more of the log.

R

Rabbit ears—Name often used in reference to the finials on a pressed back dining chair.

Raised panel—The result of a chamfer.

Reeding—Semi-circular, straight cuttings resembling reeds. A series of parallel lines of small convex or beaded mounting. The reverse of fluting.

Recessed panel—The result when cross-members are set into the stiles of a cased furniture item.

Ribbon-back—A chair back with a ribbon motif ornament.

Rolltop—Narrow, parallel slats, either rounded as a half-moon or shaped as a pyramid (on the top) and mounted on a flexible backing. Designed to roll up and down to protect a writing surface or file compartment inside the furniture piece: a self-storing flexible hood.

Roman chair—An armchair design freely adapted from a style of 16th century Italian Renaissance folding X-form, called a Dantesca.

Roundel—Round or circular ornamentation. Often found on Eastlake-style furniture items. Often referred to as "bull's eyes."

Rung—A crosspiece connecting cabinet, chair, or table legs providing structural strength. Sometimes called "stretchers" or "runners."

S

Saddle Seat—A solid seat shaped to fit the contours of the body. Most comfortable. Fondly called "bun-dips."

Saltire—A straight X-shaped stretcher.

Scalloped—A series of curves, providing an ornamental edge.

Sculptured seat—A solid seat of a chair contoured in its shape to follow the lines of the body for comfort.

Seats—The fundamental form has generally been dependent on the special purpose and on the ever-varying mode of life. The details have been influenced by the artistic taste of the time and by the materials used in construction.

In spite of the variety of forms, the height of the seat is a common feature. In order to sit comfortably, the feet should just reach the floor. The seat height therefore is from 15 to 18 inches. The depth of the seat shows greater variation, from 12 to 24 inches. The height of the back varies from 30 inches and more. The upper surface of the arms should be about 12 inches above that of the seat.

Straight, upright backs are less comfortable than curved lines adapted to the vertebral curve. Similarly, flat horizontal seats are not so comfortable as shaped, saddle seats.

Secretary desk—A combination desk with a bookcase provided above the desk.

Sectional bookcase—A design of bookcase constructed in units stacked upon one another, resting on a base and finished with a cap. Various styles and heights appear. The glass doors lift up to slide back along the inside top of each case, making access to the contents most convenient.

Serpentine—A front shaped with a waving curve or curves.

Settee—A small scale, elongated seat with a back to accomodate several persons.

Shaving stand—A tall, slender article of furniture, designed for use while shaving. An adjustable mirror of any shape stands above a small cabinet with compartments to house the straight razor and shaving supplies.

Side-by-side desk—A combination bookcase and desk in a single piece of furniture. Sometimes referred to as a "half and half." A double side-by-side offers two bookcases, usually with the desk in the center.

Sideboard—An item of furniture intended for the reception of articles used in the service of the table. They are useful for serving. Decorative vases and objects may be place upon them. They are themselves decorative objects. Larger in size than a buffet or server.

Single post backleg—A continuous vertical supporting post, providing both the rear leg and side post supporting the back. Also called "uprights," or stiles.

Skirt—see Apron.

Slat—A flat, thin, horizontal bar of wood used on chair backs and arm supports.

Slip seat—A seat capable of being removed from a chair, usually covered with leather or fabric.

Sofa or Couch—Elongated chairs, some having the character of a bed. They can be used for lying or sitting.

Spooning—A chair-back shaped to fit the contour of the body.

Splat—A central vertical member of a chair back as center back panel. Can be plain, decorated, or cut-out.

Spindle—A slender, turned, vertical baluster.

Spiral-turning—A twisted form of turning.

Splashback—A high rim at the back of a washstand to prevent splattering of the wall when using the washbowl. Sometimes called a "splashboard."

Splay legs—Slanting outward from beneath the seat of a chair for added strength and steadiness to keep it from tipping over.

Stick 'n Ball—A design of spindle work with round balls connected to one another by straight or twisted dowels. Often put together to form intricate decorative designs.

Stickley, Gustav (1857-1942)—The leading exponent of the Arts and Crafts movement in America. Greatly influenced by the English Arts and Crafts designers, Stickley visited England in 1898 to return to the United States with the idea of a new concept in American furniture designs. He abandoned his previous, rather typical furniture pursuits to experiment with his first designs in Craftsman furniture.

Stickley was searching for an honest furniture style based on structural truth and functionalism. He created solid, plain-lined furniture that appeared to have been built by hand.

Woodworking machines prepared the lumber which was then assembled, pegged, stained and finished by the workman's hand, proclaiming the principles of the Arts and Crafts movement. Quarter-sawn oak was the first choice of lumber. The dynamic flaking provided the only decoration for his new style.

Introduced to America at the 1900 Grand Rapids, Michigan Furniture Exposition, Stickley's new concept in American furniture received acclaim. Many manufacturers copied his furniture style as a result of its favorable acceptance.

Stickley named his furniture "Craftsman." The generic name "Mission," was adopted, much to his disappointment.

Stiles—The vertical or upright piece in a framed furniture item into which the secondary members are fitted.

Stool—The simplest seat which is a chair without a back. The revolving stool permits lateral movement and adjustment to different heights as required. This is effected by means of a screw.

Straight-sawn—Lumber taken from the log by slicing lengthwise, exposing the growth rings of the tree producing straight grain.

Stretcher—The underbracing of chairs, tables and other furniture, originally serving as a foot rest. Usually positioned low between the legs. Rung when higher.

T

T-back chair—The name often used to refer to the chair style that has a center vertical back panel, or splat, forming a "T".

Table—The oldest and most important piece of furniture, next to the chair. The main uses are as a dining-table, a work-table, and a fancy table on which to place vases or items for display.

The principle parts are the frame and the flat top. The top may be square, rectangular, circular, elleptical, or any variation in between. Tables may have one leg or column. When three, four, or more legs are used as supports, they are often joined by means of framework. Connecting stretchers may join the legs for rigidity. Legs are prismatic, turned or curved. They either stand upright or curve outward. Drawers may be accomodated in the framework of the table. Tables made to expand their size as an extension dining table or to fold up as a tilt-top.

Decoration is confined to the under frame, which is ornamented by carving and stylish turnings suitable to the supports. Where the top is decorated, the ornamentation if flat as incised carving.

The size of the table varies according to its purpose. The height varies little and is 28½" for ordinary tables.

Taboret, or taborette—A small plant stand.

Thornet, Michael—See Bentwood.

Tiger-oak—The contemporary name for vividly grained quarter-sawn oak either solid or usually found in veneer. Often resembles a tiger's stripes.

Top rail—The top member of a chair back; headpiece.

Turning—Shaping wood on a lathe or with chisels to form table or chair legs or spindles.

U

Upholstered chair—Where the seat and possibly the back are padded.

Upright—An extension of back legs supporting the chair back.

V

Valance—An apron or skirt used for the top of a furniture piece rather than at the base.

Veneer—A thin coating of ornamental wood permitting a display of figured grain, not possible otherwise. This is glued to the body of plain solid wood. The idea that veneered furniture is cheapened furniture has long passed as an erroneous idea. Veneered furniture represents the highest attainment of the furniture makers art.

W

Wardrobe—See *Armoire*.

Washstand—An enclosed cabinet used in the bedroom for the purpose of washing. The bowl and pitcher sat on the top with the necessary towels draped on the towel bar standing above the back. When the chamber pot is housed in the cupboard compartment, the form is referred to as a commode.

Whorl-feet—A curled up scroll or knurl.

Woven cane seat—see Cane.

Manufacturers

Of the hundreds of furniture manufacturers working in America during the turn of the century period, those listed below are well-known for their oak productions. The page references indicate illustrations in this book.

W.S. Arrow
1428 Eleventh Avenue
Altoona, PA
"Everything for the home"

Baldwin Refrigerator Co., 126
Burlington, VT

Banta Furniture Co.
Joshen, IL

S. Bent & Bros.
Gardner, MA

Burrows Bros. & Co., Ltd.
Picture Rocks, Lycoming, PA
Manufacturers of oak chamber suites, sideboards

Columbia Phonograph Co., 92, 93
New York

Crandall-Bennett Porter Co.
Mohtoursville
High grade tables

Danner

A. H. Davenport
Boston, MA

H.C. Dexter Chair Co., 176
Black River, NY

Estey Manufacturing Co., 137
Owasso, MI

Globe-Wernicke Co., 104, 106-108
Cincinnati, OH

Gunn Furniture Co., 103
Grand Rapids, MI

Gurney Refrigerator Co., 125
Ronddulac, WI

Hagerstown Furniture Co.
Hagerstown, MD
Manufacturers of tables, stand, etc.

F. E. Hale Manufacturing Co.
Herkimer, NY
Hales interchangeable bookcases

Hall Refrigerator Co.
Greenville, MI

Hastings Table Co.
Hastings, MI
Leaf locks

Herter Bros.
New York City interior designers
New York book of collectibles

Herzog Art Furniture
Saginaw—W.S. MI
"Our Art Beautifies Your Home"

Illinois Sewing Machine Co., 168
Rockford, IL
"New Royal" machine

Innis, Pearce & Co.
Rushville, IN

Johnson Chair Co., 157, 159
Chicago, IL
Signature on cast iron mechanism

Kewaunee Manufacturing Co., 122
Laboratory Furniture Experts
Kewaunee, WI

Library Bureau Solemakers, 167

Macey, 100, 105

Marstall Furniture Co., 154
Henderson, KY
Oak Wardrobes and Cupboards

Miller Cabinet Company, 173
Rochester, NY

Montgomery Table Works
Montgomery, PA

Morganton Furniture Co.
Morganton, NC
Buffets, chiffoniers, sideboards

National Furniture Co., 111
Williamsport, PA

Nelson, Matter & Co.
Lyon Street
Grand Rapids, MI
Manufacturers and wholesale and retail dealers in furniture

Pease Piano Company, 93
New York

Reaser Furniture Company, 81
Gettysburg, PA
Manufacturers

Rockford Standard Furniture Co., 41
Rockford, IL

Sleigh Furniture Co.
Grand Rapids, MI

A.C. Theriot
Philadelphia, PA
Woodcarver, furniture designer

Udell Works
Indianapolis, IN

Watsontown Table & Furniture Co., 114
Watsontown, PA
Manufacturers of extension tables

Werners Piano, Furniture, Victrolas
Easton, PA
Established 1881

H. Wisler & Son, 63
Philadelphia, PA

Bibliography

"Arts and Crafts Movement," *Encyclopedia Britannica*, 1988 ed., vol. 1.

Ayers, Marcy and Walter, *Larken Oak*, Summerdale, PA, Echo Publishing, 1984.

Blundell, Peter S. *The Marketplace Guide to Oak Furniture*, Paducah, KY, Collectors Books, 1980.

Century Furniture Company, *Furniture*, Grand Rapids, MI, Century Furniture Company, 1928.

Dubrow, Eileen and Richard, *Furniture Made in America; 1875-1905*, West Chester, PA, Schiffer Publishing Ltd., 1982.

"Edison," *Encyclopedia Britannica*, 1988 ed., vol. 17.

Feinman, Jeffrey ed. *Fall 1909 Sears, Roebuck Catalogue.* Ventura Books, Inc., New York, NY, 1979.

Grun, Bernard, *The Timetables of History*, New York, NY, Simon & Schuster, Inc., Touchtone Edition, 1982.

Isreal, Fred L. ed. *1897 Sears, Roebuck Catalogue*, New York, NY, Chelsea House Publishers, 1976.

Johnson, Bruce, *Official Identification and Price Guide to Arts and Crafts*, New York, NY, The House of Collectibles, 1988.

Kennedy, Philip D., *Hoosier Cabinets*, Indianapolis, IN, Philip D. Kennedy.

McNerney, Kathryn, *American Oak Furniture*, Paducah, KY, Collectors Books, 1984.

Meyer, Franz Sales, *Handbook of Ornament*, New York, NY, Dover Publications, Inc. 1957.

Morningstar, Connie, "Dining Room Furniture of the 1880's," *Spinning Wheel*, 423, May/June, 1982.

Schiffer, Nancy N., *America's Oak Furniture*, West Chester, PA, Schiffer Publishing Ltd., 1989.

Schroeder, Joseph J, ed. *1908 Sears, Roebuck Catalogue*, Northfield, IL, Digest Books Inc., 1971.

Schroeder, Joseph J. ed, *Fall 1900 Sears, Roebuck and Company Catalogue*, Northfield, IL, DBI Books, Inc., a subsidiary of Technical Publishing Co., 1970.

Stickley Craftsman Furniture Catalogs; Craftsman Furniture Made by Gustav Stickley and *The Work of L. & L.G. Stickley*, Introduction by David M. Cathers, NY, Dover Publications, Inc., 1979.

Sutcliff, G. Lester, ed., *Heritage of Styles and Essential Woods.* (The Modern Carpenter Joiner and Cabinet-Maker Series). The National Historical Society, 1990.

Swedberg, Robert W. and Harriette, *American Oak Furniture*, Radnor, PA, Wallace-Homestead Book Company, 1982 Revised edition, 1986.

Time-Life Books, *Oak Furniture.* (The Encyclopedia of Collectibles Series), Alexandria, VA, Time Life Books, Inc., 1979.

INDEX

DECORATIVE ARTS & DESIGN

ARCHITECTURE

The Farm, An American Living Portrait Joan and David Hagan. Images of country life are captured; glimpses of everyday chores reverently preserved. The bountiful land, the architecture it spawned, and the lives of the people, animals, and crops it supports. Hundreds of color photographs relate heart-warming moments, beautiful landscapes, personalities, and architectural details which make up farm life everywhere.
Size: 8 1/2" x 11"   160 pp.
ISBN: 0-88740-259-3   soft cover $29.95

American Barns Stanley Schuler. In this handsomely printed volume, 240 barns throughout the United States: huge barns and small barns; Pennsylvania Dutch barns and New England barns; horse barns and carriage houses, and countless others are presented with gorgeous pictures and explanations. 113 color plates   186 b/w photos
Size: 8 1/2" x 11"   224 pp.
ISBN: 0-88740-145-7   soft cover $24.95

Shaker Architecture Herbert Schiffer. Each of the Shaker communities is represented with very interesting photographs of the buildings that made up their world. Many modern designs have their roots in Shaker tradition.
282 b/w photographs
Size: 8 1/2" x 11"   Index   190 pp.
ISBN: 0-88740-153-8   soft cover $24.95

Shaker Village Edmund V. Gillon, Jr. The village consists of six cut-and-assemble architectural models in H-O scale, printed on heavy stock in full color. Includes great round stone barn, four-story brick communal dwelling, schoolhouse, gambrel-roof church, laundry, and privy. Has brief history of Shakers in America, a description of the buildings, and instructions for assembly.   Size: 9" x 12"   46 pp.
ISBN: 0-88740-077-9   soft cover $5.95

Early Domestic Architecture of Pennsylvania Eleanor Raymond. The pictures and architectural drawings include numerous illustrations of outbuildings, pumps, spring houses, and barns.
Size: 8 1/2" x 11"   158 pp.
297 b/w photographs   177 line drawings
ISBN: 0-916838-11-0   hard cover $29.95

An Early New England Seaport Edmund V. Gillon, Jr. This cut-and-assemble book contains ten architectural models in H-O scale, printed in full color on sturdy stock. The authentic buildings are representative of the types that existed in late 18th and 19th century waterfronts of such famous New England seaports as Salem, Nantucket, New Bedford, Newburyport, and New London.
18 color photos   22 b/w photos
Size: 9" x 12"   56 pp.
ISBN: 0-88740-063-9   soft cover $5.95

Old New England Homes Stanley Schuler. Colonial, Georgian, Federal, and Victorian homes are presented with an informative and readable text. Floor plans are given for many of the homes, and the 225 color pictures show several angles of the buildings plus frontal views.
Size: 8 1/2" x 11"   224 pp.
213 b/w photographs   225 color photographs
ISBN: 0-88740-034-5   hard cover $35.00

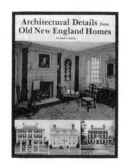

Architectural Details from Old New England Homes (Revised) Stanley Schuler. Over 350 color and black-and-white photographs and supporting text show and explain variations in architectural styles of old New England homes. Architectural drawings provide close-up views of fireplaces, doorways, windows, stairs, and cupboards built in the 17th, 18th, and 19th centuries.
Size: 8 1/2" x 11"   Index   144 pp.
14 color plates   160 b/w photographs
ISBN: 0-7643-0280-7   soft cover $29.95

Saltbox and Cape Cod Houses Stanley Schuler. Homes in traditional Saltbox and Cape Cod styles are being built all over America because the designs embody a practical and unassuming charm. Hundreds of examples of old traditional styles and newer adaptations in color photos. Since the 1600s, the uncomplicated, sensible two-storyfloor plans of both of these New England types have endeared them to home builders.   144 color photographs   132 b/w photos
Size: 8 1/2" x 11"   7 floor plans   160 pp.
ISBN: 0-88740-156-2   hard cover $29.95

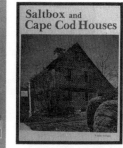

The Cape Cod House Stanley Schuler. There are many floor plans and photographs presented to help those who want to build their own Cape Cod houses. Examples range from tiny single style to double, triple, modified, and "modern" interpretations. 14 color plates 160 b/w photos
Size: 8 1/2" x 11"   Index   144 pp.
ISBN: 0-916838-63-3   hard cover $25.00

Provincetown Discovered Edward V. Gillon. This photographic record of Provincetown, Mass. captures some of New England's best seascapes and architecture. Many charming eighteenth-century Cape Cod houses and splendid Greek Revival homes of the 1850s to 1900 and churches, commercial buildings and farm-related structures are shown with excellent detailed pictures.
Size: 8 1/2" x 11"   124 b/w photos   127 pp.
ISBN: 0-88740-061-2   soft cover $12.95

Mississippi Valley Architecture: Houses of the Lower Mississippi Valley Stanley Schuler. Artful photos give a broad view of houses in the lower Mississippi River Valley. These magnificent homes reflect diverse cultural backgrounds and adaptations to this scenic river valley. Schuler traces the use of the French Colonial, Greek Revival, and vernacular styles in each region. Facades, floor plans, and details of homes built between 1700 and the Civil War.
Size: 8 1/2" x 11"   5 maps   240 pp.
97 color plates, floor plans   248 b/w photos
ISBN: 0-916838-96-X   hard cover $30.00

SCULPTURE & ART

Contemporary Stone Sculpture Dona Z. Meilach. An exploration of modern stone sculpture, with hundreds of examples by today's top sculptors, illustrated and explained with hundreds of clearly detailed photographs. Specific, step-by-step instructions for creating stone sculpture are given, with descriptions of various types of stone, how to select and transport it, how to carve the stone with hand tools and electric or pneumatic power tools, and the methods of finishing the work.
17 color plates 340 illustrations
Size: 7" x 10"   Index   224 pp.
ISBN: 0-88740-089-2   soft cover $24.95

Direct Stone Sculpture Milt Liebson. After a historical overview of stone sculpture, the reader is lead through the hands-on experience of sculpting in stone. The types of stone used are covered, as are the types and use of basic hand sculpting tools. For the advanced sculptor, there is detailed information on the use of power tools, methods of lamination, repair, the business side of stone sculpture, and more.
Size 8 1/2" x 11"   160 pp.
ISBN: 0-88740-305-0   hard cover $29.95

Art Bronzes Michael Forrest. An important and lavishly beautiful study of the discovery, appreciation, recognition, and selection of fine bronze statuary created during the 19th and early 20th centuries. Over 1100 illustrations, 200 in full color, and many pages of carefully researched text with relevant marks, inscriptions, artist signatures, dates, and foundry stamps. Over 450 artists are represented.

Size: 9" x 12"   Index   493 pp.
200 color, 800 b/w photos About 100 drawings
ISBN: 0-88740-122-8   hard cover $95.00

The Bronzes of the Nineteenth Century: Dictionary of Sculptors Pierre Kjellberg. This complete encyclopedia of almost 750 nineteenth century French sculptors including the giants Rodin, Barye, d'Angers and Carpeaux, with biographies, listings of works (along with size and foundry when known), museum pieces in France and elsewhere, and recent sales. Also provides an overview of 19th century bronze sculpture, the foundries that cast the bronzes, and methods used to cast works.

Size: 9" x 12"   1000 photos   685pp.
ISBN: 0-88740-629-7   hard cover $150.00

1886 Catalog of the French Bronze Foundry of F. Barbedienne of Paris A reprint of the original 1886 catalog of bronzes from the House of Barbedienne one of the foremost French foundries is reproduced with original selling prices in French francs and dimensions plus the line drawings which depict many of these famous works.
Size: 8 1/2" x 11"   96pp.
ISBN: 0-88740-705-6 $14.95

Catalog of the Society des Beaux Arts, Paris. This nineteenth century catalog of the Society des Beaux Arts of Paris displays a wide variety of bronze editions of the successful sculptures of the period. An index lists the prices set for these pieces by the Society, providing fascinating insight into the nineteenth century art market.
Size: 11" x 8 1/2"   94pp.
ISBN: 0-88740-706-4 $19.95

Maxfield Parrish Coy Ludwig. This compendium of the life and work of Maxfield Parrish, is an essential part of a Parrish library. Examples are shown of Parrish's most famous book illustrations, his magazine covers, and landscapes he painted for calendars. Parrish's materials, favorite methods, and unique way of painting are examined in depth. Maxfield Parrish, Jr. explains step-by-step his father's glazing technique and use of photography in his work. An independent value guide to Parrish prints is included.
Size: 9" x 12"   64 full-color plates; over 100 black- and-white illustrations   224 pp.
ISBN: 0-88740-527-4   hard cover $39.95

BRONZES: Sculptors & Founders 1800 - 1930 by Harold Berman. This four volume set is the classic reference for commercial bronze sculptures from 1800 to 1930. Showing the works of a vast array of international sculptors and dozens of founders, with pictures so clear that even small details on the sculptures are visible.

Volume 1: Has essay on specific topics of identification and caring for bronze.
Size: 8 1/2" x 11"   799 photos   224 pp.
ISBN: 088740-700-5 $79.95

Volume 2:   Size: 8 1/2' x 11"
1025 photographs   272 pp.
ISBN: 088740-701-3 $79.95

Volume 3: Volume 3, in addition to photographs of works by artists and foundries from throughout the international community, provides detailed information on the Hirsch Foundry of Paris and Brooklyn, NY and contains important listing of Canadian sculptors.
Size: 8 1/2" x 11"   1315 photos   320 pp.
ISBN: 088740-702-1 $79.95

Volume 4: Includes 43 sculptures recently made by the Hirsch Foundry of Paris and Brooklyn, New York from nineteenth century molds.
Size: 8 1/2" x 11"
1735 photos   400 pp.
ISBN: 088740-703-X
$79.95

INDEX to VOLUMES 1,2,3 & 4; Provides a complete listing by artist for all four volumes and identifies the location of photographs and full information in the series. $20.00
ISBN: 0-88740-704-8   Size: 8 1/2" x 11"